ROUTLEDGE LIBRARY EDITIONS
BROADCASTING

Volume 32

TEACHERS & TELEVISION

TEACHERS & TELEVISION

ERNEST CHOAT,
HARRY GRIFFIN
AND
DOROTHY HOBART

LONDON AND NEW YORK

First published in 1987 by Croom Helm

This edition first published in 2024
by Routledge
4 Park Square, Milton Park, Abingdon, Oxon OX14 4RN

and by Routledge
605 Third Avenue, New York, NY 10158

Routledge is an imprint of the Taylor & Francis Group, an informa business

© 1987 Ernest Choat and Harry Griffin

All rights reserved. No part of this book may be reprinted or reproduced or utilised in any form or by any electronic, mechanical, or other means, now known or hereafter invented, including photocopying and recording, or in any information storage or retrieval system, without permission in writing from the publishers.

Trademark notice: Product or corporate names may be trademarks or registered trademarks, and are used only for identification and explanation without intent to infringe.

British Library Cataloguing in Publication Data
A catalogue record for this book is available from the British Library

ISBN: 978-1-032-59391-3 (Set)
ISBN: 978-1-032-64394-6 (Volume 32) (hbk)
ISBN: 978-1-032-64400-4 (Volume 32) (pbk)
ISBN: 978-1-032-64397-7 (Volume 32) (ebk)

DOI: 10.4324/9781032643977

Publisher's Note
The publisher has gone to great lengths to ensure the quality of this reprint but points out that some imperfections in the original copies may be apparent.

Disclaimer
The publisher has made every effort to trace copyright holders and would welcome correspondence from those they have been unable to trace.

TEACHERS & TELEVISION

ERNEST CHOAT, HARRY GRIFFIN
AND DOROTHY HOBART

CROOM HELM
London • New York • Sydney

© 1987 Ernest Choat and Harry Griffin
Croom Helm Ltd, Provident House, Burrell Row,
Beckenham, Kent, BR3 1AT

Croom Helm Australia, 44-50 Waterloo Road,
North Ryde, 2113, New South Wales

Published in the USA by
Croom Helm
in association with Methuen, Inc.
29 West 35th Street,
New York, NY 10001

British Library Cataloguing in Publication Data

Choat, Ernest
   Teachers and Television.
   1. Television in education
   I Title II. Griffin, Harry   III. Hobart, Dorothy
   371.3′358   LB1044.7
   ISBN 0-7099-4819-0

Library of Congress Cataloging-in-Publication Data

ISBN 0-7099-4819-0

Printed and bound in Great Britain
by Billing & Sons Limited, Worcester.

CONTENTS

		Pages
Acknowledgements		vii
List of tables		ix
List of figures		xi
1	Young Children, Teachers and Educational Television	1
2	How Evaluation was Conducted	28
3	Teachers Using Television	38
4	Teachers' Reactions Towards Television	73
5	Pre-school Children, Teachers and Television	84
6	Television and Curriculum Content	100
7	Implications, Change and Future Development	119
Appendices		138
Index		152

ACKNOWLEDGEMENTS

We are grateful to the Leverhulme Trust for funding the Incorporating Educational Television into the Curriculum up to the Age of Seven Years Project and to Dr. Ronald Tress for his advice in the early stages of the work. We must also thank the Independent Broadcasting Authority and Thames TV for the donations made towards expenses for 1983/84, and the DES for 1984/85.

We are indebted to the University of London Institute of Education for accommodating us, and particularly thank Professor Denis Lawton, Professor Harvey Goldstein, Dr. Peter Dean and Bob Ferguson for their support. We also valued immensely the co-operation and assistance given by Pascal Kivotos, Head of the AVE Centre, University of London Goldsmith's College.

However, the research would not have been possible without the teacher participants, and we must thank all those who monitored educational television series and completed pro formas and questionnaires in both the pilot work and main study. Much of this work would not have been completed without co-operation of the Local Education Authority Inspectors/Advisers and the willingness and enthusiasm of the group leaders who arranged the distribution and collection of the research material, and acted as chairpersons at the in-service sessions. We are most grateful for all that they did.

Our work was made easier by the services of an excellent secretary, Sheila Moger, for most of the project. Her efficiency, cheerful disposition and the care she took of us made our task that much easier. Unfortunately, she left during the compilation of this book but we thank her for the typing and preparation which she did and her successor, Pat Hollingshead, who gallantly completed a complex and awkward task.

Dr. Ernest Choat (Director)
Harry Griffin (Research Fellow)
Dorothy Hobart (Research Fellow)

TABLES

Table		Pages
2.1	Classes taught according to age-range of children	34
2.2	The educational television series monitored by the teachers and the number of instances of use for language, mathematics and general interest	36
3.1	Organisation of children's viewing according to number of teachers	47
3.2	The number of occasions other activities were pursued after programmes	56
3.3	Distinction of programme use between direct follow-up and other activities	64
3.4	Teachers' estimations of whether or not their anticipated learning outcomes through using educational television series had been achieved	66
4.1	Number of teachers and the type of receiver they used to view educational television series	74
4.2	Means and organisation of children to view educational television	77
4.3	How the teachers considered educational television affected the curriculum	81
4.4	The teachers' views on what were considered the greatest benefits children obtain from watching educational television	82
5.1	The means of viewing television for those nursery teachers who had the facility available	84
5.2	The number of television series used by the nursery teachers	87

FIGURES

Figures		Pages
2.1	Plan of Phase II of the Project	30
3.1	Introductory remarks and terms used in the teachers' booklets relating to follow-up and associated activities	58
3.2	How programme content was used with further activities	62
4.1	The facilities which teachers would like to be more extensively provided by the possession of a video recorder.	76

CHAPTER ONE

YOUNG CHILDREN, TEACHERS AND EDUCATIONAL TELEVISION

The National Association of Head Teachers (1983 p.19) refer to television as the most powerful medium of mass communication man has invented, and they point out that it has tremendous potential as an educational tool if used carefully and with professional thought. These are admirable sentiments, but to what extent are head teachers and teachers considering educational television as a component of the curriculum? As the NAHT (op cit) state, it is head teachers and teachers who decide which programmes shall be seen, when they shall be seen and by whom.
The ITV companies began educational television broadcasts for infants' schools in 1964, and the British Broadcasting Corporation followed three years later. Four series, Watch (BBC), Words and Pictures (BBC), Seeing and Doing (Thames) and My World (Yorkshire) were being broadcast by 1970 until, in 1983/84, the output had increased to eleven series, ITV (six series) and BBC (five series, although a further series 'Look and Read' which is intended for junior school children, is taken by many infants' schools). Nevertheless, limited research has been carried out in Britain into the use of educational television, particularly as it relates to children up to the age of seven years. The School Broadcasting Council, Independent Broadcasting Authority and individual television companies conduct surveys through their Education Officers and research personnel, but the findings are not usually made public. The IBA also publish the results of one-year fellowships which they offer for teachers to enquire into an aspect of broadcasting.
A substantial enquiry was conducted in 1972/1973 by C.G. Hayter, a retired HMI, on behalf

YOUNG CHILDREN, TEACHERS AND EDUCATIONAL TELEVISION

of the BBC and IBA. Hayter (1974) set up his study with a simple hypothesis - a school interested in and willing to explore the planned use of broadcasts, together with a realistic level of equipment, could achieve distinctive educational gains for its pupils. He collected material from one hundred and six schools through case studies and reports from head teachers and teachers, and focussed on eleven schools (primary and secondary) to report on the success of the experiment. Hayter showed what could be done with schools that had attention and support, but did not examine what was happening in thousands of other schools that were without the special facilities. This is emphasised by Wade and Poole (1983) when they state that it is clear that educational television is an important aid to the teacher but what is less clear, even after many years of provision, are the particular ways children respond to it and the specific effects of broadcasts. They suggest there is a need for more evaluative research; a plea which was made in the report on the future of broadcasting - the Annan Report (1977 p.304), and also in the Bullock Report (1975 pp. 322-327) which complained of a lack of money to carry out research and believed it was time for such to be undertaken, and many years earlier by Himmelweit, Oppenheim and Vince (1958 pp. 64-66).

Apart from the Bullock Report's recommendation for the use of educational television in language development and its belief that "teachers should continue to be provided with this valuable source of stimulus for talking, reading and writing", other official reports have recognised the existence of educational television but provided limited guidance on its use with young children. The Plowden Report (1967) stated television was part of ordinary life and that children should be taught to use it profitably and associate it with learning as well as entertainment, but the Primary School Survey (1978) made only passing remarks, and the Cockcroft Report (1982) merely added that mathematics programmes can form the basis of a course or supplement other work. The First School Survey (1982) was critical of the way many teachers were using educational television, but the HMIs did not suggest what should be done to overcome the deficiencies. Likewise, books have been published which theorize on the education of young children but omit to consider educational television. Dearden (1976) deals with the practical problems of primary education, but does not include educational television. Pluckrose (1979) examines the content of the primary school curriculum and the philosophy which underlies it but educational television is excluded. Blenkin and Kelly (1981) discuss the characteristics of 'progressive' education in primary schools and the definition of education and curriculum in terms of process, but no mention is made of the role of educational television in the considerations.

Local education authorities also pay scant attention to educational television in their curriculum recommendations. The Inner London Education Authority (1981 pp. 2-5) state that the primary school curriculum should consist of three fundamental elements - language; mathematics; and aesthetic development with physical education - together with those areas of experience, knowledge, attitude and skills which depend for their definition and extension on the skills embodied in the previous three categories. According to the ILEA, "such a curriculum demands a style of teaching that is highly organised yet sufficiently flexible for the groupings of children to vary from individual to group to the whole class, in which the time scale allotted to the work in hand can vary from child to child and from task to task". Ninety seven per cent of primary schools are equipped with television receivers and possession of video recorders is rapidly increasing (Educational Broadcasting Council 1982) quoted by (Bates 1984 p.35). This take-up indicates that educational television should be central to curriculum considerations but no allowance is made for this. Essex County Council (1983) produced a curriculum document on the significance of topics and centres of interest to children's developmental needs and interests but did not appraise inclusion of the medium when suggesting guidelines to establish a school's policy in this area of the curriculum.

Irrespective of the oversight of educational television in official publications, claims are made that recommend its use with young children. McCreesh and Maher (1976 pp. 87-88) believe that the value of television as a resource for young children lies in its potential for linking experience to language, helping children to formulate ideas, to stimulate their thinking, and presenting a valuable dimension of the world in which they live. Kirby (1981 p. 41) considers television as a means for giving young children acquaintance with a world beyond their immediate experience, providing the impressions gained are discussed with an understanding adult.

YOUNG CHILDREN, TEACHERS AND EDUCATIONAL TELEVISION

Lesser (1972) maintains that one of television's great powers is its capacity to transport, to show the world to children - to display people, events and ideas that they have never encountered before and are unlikely ever to have the opportunity to confront in person.
Although educational television has been largely neglected within curriculum considerations, its existence and possible contribution to young children's education has been acknowledged by others. Some people go to the extent of stating that young children can and do learn from television, i.e. Lesser (ibid), Bryant, Alexander and Brown (1983), and Home (1983), and Fowles and Horner (1974) even insist that an American series Sesame Street has proved that children not only learn from television but that active interaction is not always necessary for learning. Lesser (op. cit) contends that television is a vehicle for direct teaching by telling and showing what is intended children should learn, then teaching them by telling and showing it to them, and finally by telling and showing them again what they have been taught. This contention is reinforced by Fowles and Voyat (1974) who maintain that television facilitates rote verbal learning and they refute those educators who consider the medium to be "a passive learning tool in that the learning that goes on will generally take an imitative mode".
Most of these comments on learning from television are American and orientated towards skill acquisition through Sesame Street and a further series The Electric Company. Commenting on these series, Williams (1981) adds that there is some evidence that children can learn skills from them, i.e. Ball and Bogatz (1970), Bogatz and Ball (1971), Corteen (1977), Gadberry (1980), Morgan (1980), and Salomon (1976). Commenting on the importation of Sesame Street into Israel, Salomon (loc cit) states that the overall effect was clear: although there were social class and age differences, children of all age groups learned what the series' designers declared it was intended to teach them. However, only seven and eight-year-olds showed improved skill mastery. Five-year-olds, even when heavily exposed to the series, did not show any improvement in skill mastery and were far below the seven and eight-year-olds in their comprehension level. Salomon suggests that age, or perhaps cognitive development, appeared to be a crucial factor in these results - a fact which is comparable to other findings. The magnitude

of the effects of Sesame Street has been questioned by Cook and Connor (1976) and Sprigle (1972), while Levinsohn (1977) asks whether television can be used to teach the basic skills. She feels that it is inevitable and only a question of time before some of the responsibility for teaching the three Rs will be given to television producers.

As the earlier contentions imply, there is a widespread body of opinion which assumes that television can teach and children will thereby learn, but individuals are required to analyse when television is used for direct teaching. They interpret what they see and hear through abstractions based on past experience. Television may provide language lessons to watch and listen to, present mathematical notions desirable to acquire, and show examples of the Roman way of life to stimulate a topic, but such broadcasts demand reasoning at a formal level of operations. Young children have not reached the stage of mental development to apply abstract reasoning to deduce and rationalize from indirect experience. Much of what young children are required to learn in school can be shown on television, but it is questionable whether they do learn from it. They are not at a stage in their intellectual development to connect many explanations seen on television with reality (Choat 1983a, Choat, Griffin and Hobart 1983). Prolonged exposure of children to television cannot create its own order of understanding. Young children cannot make the jump in logical deduction no matter how realistically events are portrayed in a television programme. They need a means to interpret what is seen and heard. No child can be a 'television restricted' child. He must encounter real life situations which supplement his exposure to television, irrespective of these real life situations being extremely limited (Choat 1984).

Noble (1975 pp. 83-84) suggests that egocentrism in thought is likely to colour young children's television viewing in five distinct ways. First, a young child is likely to think in a binary way, i.e. he will respond in an all-or-nothing manner to television. He cannot be expected to perceive shades of grey in television characters: they will be perceived as either all good or all bad. Secondly, the child is unable to perceive events from any point of view other than his own. Therefore, young children may be expected to consider television as reality because they are not capable of imagining that people can act dramatic parts. Similarly, both puppets and cartoon characters are likely to be thought of as real and alive, having an existence independent of the screen. Thirdly, egocentrism in thought should lead young children to imagine that either he or his friends are involved in television programmes. All external events occur because of their intervention and they are likely to think that they influence the events which take place on the television screen. Fourthly, young children classify objects and events, both on and off television, in unique ways. An object is defined by its location and when a scene changes in a television film and a character appears in a new situation, or as smaller or larger than before, the person may be seen as a different person or puppet than the one previously seen. Fifthly, because young children cannot use operations in thought they are unable to reverse the constituents in a chain of reasoning. It would seem reasonable, therefore, to expect that young children, who cannot reverse operations, are unlikely to recall the beginning of a television programme, nor be able to predict what will happen next. They will not perceive that a television programme has a beginning, a middle and an end.

These deliberations suggest that young children at the pre-operational stage of mental and thought development do not fully comprehend the sequence and motives of television programmes, have fewer analytical abilities and have insufficient experience of the world to interpret, understand and critically appreciate a television broadcast, but an adult watching with them can have an impact on their understanding of programmes. Corder-Bolz (1980) goes to the extent of stating that as parents and other adults verbalize their interpretations and evaluations of television programmes to children, the children will internalize these critical viewing skills which can ultimately make television a more positive part of their lives.

The question therefore is whether young children do learn from television and, if so, what is the type of learning? Children looking at a television receiver are not necessarily processing the information portrayed. Many adults assume that children are interpreting from television as they do themselves, but this is a mistaken premise, and, in ths connection, Bates (Bliss, Goater, Jones and Bates 1983) raises an important question when he asks whether the kind of thinking stimulated or reinforced by the way information is coded and presented on television is closer to one stage of Piaget's stages of development of thought than another. He suggests that this seems closer to the concrete operational stage rather than the formal operational stage, but Choat (1984) asks what about educational television for those children at the pre-operational stage, i.e. children up to six or seven years of age in terms of mental development? What form should educational television take, and how does it affect the learning of these children who have not reached the level which Bliss (op. cit) describes as "an integrated and coherent system of mental operations with which they will be able to organise the world around them"?

It does appear that children are increasingly able to focus on important or central information in a television programme as their thought processes develop. Collins, Wellman, Keniston and Westby (1978) indicated increasing attention to content central to a plot throughout the primary school years. Calvert and Watkins (1979) concluded that four to five-year-olds recalled more incidental than central information, while the opposite held true for eight to nine-year-olds. Notwithstanding these data, Williams (1981) stated that whatever the theoretical perspective, it is clear that much of what is portrayed on the television screen is not understood by young children. He acknowledged an increase in learning of both central and peripheral material up to adolescence, but emphasised that there have been very few studies of children under the age of about eight years. This is important because (a) young children's viewing patterns are such that it is difficult to imagine them learning much information central to a theme or plot, (b) young children are unable to understand sequencing, motives and consequences, (c) television broadcasts for preoperational children are detached from actuality until translated into experience by some other object, event, person, etc., and (d) Williams' (ibid) contention that children's learning is affected both by content and by experience allied to the cognitive capacity to understand not only the content but also the techniques of the medium.

Bates (1983; 1981) puts the matter into perspective when he alleges that there seems to be so little research or literature on the issue that it is tempting to ask, "Is the process of learning from television different from learning from other media?" Bates considers Salomon's (1979) work the most relevant in the area but feels that apart from some convincing work on the relationship between television and perceptual skills, even this is at best vague about the relationship between specific media and the process of learning and thinking. According to Bates (op. cit), the misapprehension can be attributed to a lack of distinction between teaching and learning. He considers that there is a need to distinguish teaching (which is more concerned with selection, presentation, representation and prior structuring of knowledge or experiences by the teacher) from learning (which is more concerned with the perception, interpretation and relating of knowledge or experience by the learner). Thus media, which present and represent knowledge, are used by teachers as ways of presenting knowledge, but media affect learners; a medium relates in different ways to teachers (and teaching) and learners (and learning).

Although Bates makes this vital distinction, there remains a great deal of confusion as to what the writers are implying when they refer to learning from educational television. They do not specify what they mean. Choat (1980 p. 92; 1981) states that learning is a measurable change in an individual that involves either the acquisition of some new body of information (cognitive learning) or a shift in values, attitudes, interest or motivation (non-cognitive learning). Consequently, learning may cover many different activities irrespective of having the common characteristic of a change in behaviour. According to Thoules (1969), these are the acquisition of information by logical remembering, the acquisition of certain bodily skills, the acquisition of intellectual skills, and the acquisition of a certain group of desirable or obligatory attitudes that include aesthetic, social and moral attitudes.

How then do pre-operational children translate what they see and hear on an educational television programme and what kinds of learning is it possible to bring about? Communication is established with a television set through visual literacy which Debes (1969 pp. 25-27) describes as a group of vision-competencies developed by a human being through seeing and integrating other sensory experiences. These competencies enable a person to discriminate and interpret natural or man-made visual actions, objects and symbols encountered in his environment. Visual literacy therefore is possible only when children are able to apply their own individual perceptions of the world to a visual presentation

YOUNG CHILDREN, TEACHERS AND EDUCATIONAL TELEVISION

(Amey 1976 pp. 15-23). It is one thing to present messages on television, but are they reinforced by what a child experiences in the world around him? Visual literacy implies incorporation within the whole of the child's experiences. Visual symbols cannot be conceived as being separate from his social, emotional, physical and intellectual experiences. This suggests that educational television programmes for young children should relate in some way to experiences they have acquired, but to comply with such a requisite is a complex task for programme producers and teachers.

Nevertheless, both content and programme structure need to be commensurate with what children can cope. Programmes should have some basis whereby children can relate them to past experience and this is not easy when catering for a large and diverse audience. Secondly, it is fundamental that both producers and teachers bear in mind that educational television should not be regarded as a medium for direct teaching and learning. An intermediary is necessary between a television programme and young children and this materialises in the person of the teacher; how she incorporates the medium into the curriculum, and how she abides by the psychology of learning to promote motivation and the fulfilment of children's needs and interests. In other words, children at the pre-operational stage of mental development are not capable of logically analysing and understanding what they see and hear from an educational television programme but depend on their teacher to provide the necessary interpretation of where it fits into their experience. As Choat (1984) remarks, children may comment on aspects that they have seen or heard in a programme but this does not indicate they have learned from it. They will most likely comment on peripheral or incidental material. For example, the children may be shown cows being milked, the milk passing through the sterilizing plant and the bottling procedure in a programme, but there should not be a preconceived intention that they will assimilate the whole milking process, and neither should it be assumed they will acquire conservation of discontinuous quantities. Pre-operational children find it difficult to reason in terms of any sort of generalisation (Bliss 1983). The picture is not coherent but still being pieced together. They will not necessarily see the links a producer attempts to portray. Because of their egocentricity, isolated incidents which have a bearing to them, and which are probably allied to past experience, may be remembered, but this does not imply that such incidents become part of their body of knowledge. It may be some months or even years before a specific incident can be recalled to become an experience accommodated in a particular schema.

Educational television broadcasts for young children are detached from actuality until they are translated into experience and teachers control the regulating mechanism by providing activities and opportunities to participate in real life situations or to undertake experiments. Alternatively, teachers may resort to exchanges through language, pictorial forms or books but these are symbolic representations which rely on past experience to interpret meanings, and even meanings do not necessarily imply understanding. Consequently, as Van Hoose (1978) points out, the success of an educational television series is contingent upon imaginative, sensitive teaching. The series may provide the mind-capturing stimulus, but the teacher has to help young children to interpret and internalize the messages within each programme. As Salzberger-Wittenberg, Henry and Osborne (1983 pp.ix-x) state, we learn about the world and ourselves from the moment we are born and continue to do so throughout our lives. Our learning, in infancy and for a considerable period, takes place within a dependent relationship to other human beings. Teachers play a very important part in this: they provide a framework which either assists or hinders emotional and mental growth - and this is particularly true with educational television.

It would appear that teachers of children up to seven years of age are in a somewhat different position in their use of educational television than teachers of older children. They cannot switch on a television set and expect children to diagnose the content of a broadcast as they would themselves. The children rely on their teacher's expertise to make the broadcast meaningful and this implies that teachers have two important functions: to provide an intelligible framework to enable understanding of what is viewed, and to develop a critical awareness of the limitations and distortions of the medium as it may affect children. Teachers of young children therefore should not isolate educational television from other curriculum considerations. A television broadcast should be part of the children's normal school day. It should have an integral place in a teacher's provisions and slot into the intended activities for the children.

YOUNG CHILDREN, TEACHERS AND EDUCATIONAL TELEVISION

The preparation-broadcast-follow-up technique can over-emphasise a programme and separate it from children's normal activities causing them to be abandoned in order to concentrate on a special display. When educational television is incorporated into the curriculum preparation is embedded within the activities prior to the programme and follow-on is absorbed within the continuation of the activities. This implies that follow-on according to the activities is a more favoured approach than follow-up. Follow-on can be geared to the level of development, needs and interests of the children, whereas follow-up is a blanket approach which is apt to overlook these factors.

Thus, teachers of young children have an equally positive role to play when using educational television as they have in the rest of their teaching, and should recognise the medium as a component of the curriculum (Choat, Griffin and Hobart 1984). This is reiterated by Goddard, Hannah and Mitchell (1972 p. 8) who feel there are now so many programmes available for young children on radio and television that a careful selection is needed so that programmes chosen as suitable can be followed-on in the classroom and linked with other work which is developing. Moreover, Goddard et al contend that it is best to keep viewing groups as small as possible when planning television viewing. This is not easy if there is only one television receiver in a school but groups need not be too large if full use is made of programme repeats and video recordings. Goddard et al also suggest that it may be possible to allow a group of children to watch a programme with a supernumerary teacher who, if she is working closely with the class, can be responsible for preparation and follow-up with the group. Bailey (1973) also states that the use of all series calls for careful educational thinking and preparation: but there are some contexts where organisation and planning for use with a selected group is important. This may arise out of the recognised relevance of some units of broadcasts for the work or interests of particular children; or the need for such planning may be fundamental to a series' purpose. Thus, Bailey quotes as an example Look and Read which calls for forming a special group of children of varying chronological ages with reading difficulties.

The crucial factor which determines a teacher's approach to educational television is her interpretation of the curriculum. Kerr (1968 pp. 11-37) refers to curriculum as all learning planned and guided by the school whether it is carried out individually, in groups or as a class both inside and outside the school, and he suggests that it be divided into four inter-related components - objectives, knowledge, learning experiences, and evaluation. But Lawton (1973 pp.11-12) considers that Kerr stretches his definition somewhat farther than might appear at first sight into a model which appears possibly too complicated for translation into practice by teachers. A more precise explanation is given by Dean (1983 pp. 32-34) who, while acknowledging the many studies on curriculum in recent years, prefers to define curriculum as referring to all the learning a child does in any aspect of school life and sub-divides this into three kinds of activity which might be described as curriculum - (a) The taught curriculum (the usual meaning of the word curriculum) which covers the teaching and learning that goes on intentionally and deliberately within the classroom and elsewhere during the school day - the work which those outside the school recognise as being what the school is in business to do. (b) The institutional curriculum which includes social learning, personal development, attitudes, responsibility, and leadership by teaching those within a school about its way of life, its tasks, its values and codes of behaviour, and so on. (c) The hidden curriculum which is those parts of what children learn at school that are not only hidden from them but also from teachers. Many of the things which now might be listed under the institutional curriculum were once part of the hidden curriculum, and since this is by definition, hidden, a school cannot control it.

Dean's explanation concurs with Choat (1980 pp.21-24) when he states there is a need to consider two important aspects (a) why certain things are taught in the primary school and (b) the purpose of the curriculum. He maintains that the aim should be to offer experiences to children that, through conceptualization, will develop understanding to cope sensibly with life. A deeper purpose is that the taught curriculum should explain their world to children. Educational television can play an important role in this purpose providing its use is such that young children are able to make the necessary interpretations. This view is supported by the IBA (1978) which states that both teachers and pupils gain much more from educational broadcasts

YOUNG CHILDREN, TEACHERS AND EDUCATIONAL TELEVISION

when the programmes are used as part of a carefully planned curriculum rather than when they are used as casual additions. Meanwhile, Hayter (1974 p.61), commenting on the effects of his work, adds that rethinking on the part of teachers, individually and in groups, as to how they might best use broadcasts increasingly involved them in consideration of the whole educative process within the classroom and within the school. Robinson (1981) also feels that educational broadcasting should be fitted into a curricula framework so that it is seen to be vital and relevant and not as a desirable but, in the end, disposable extra, while Oakley (1981) adds that as most schools use television broadcasts daily as a resource to aid the development of language and reading skills in young children, it goes without saying that the material should be used in such a way that maximum involvement, learning and enjoyment take place.

Haigh (1983), however, has contrary views on the use of educational television in the curriculum. He feels that broadcasting has largely ceased to be a significantly different kind of resource, making organisational demands and giving a special aura, and argues that it is now on the way to becoming one resource among many in the multi-media progressive classroom with a didactic role of bringing into school material which the teacher will not provide. He alleges that teachers now like to think they are less dominant in classrooms and that they evoke rather than demand responses from children, but television continues to remain an instrument of domination. Haigh contends that the only sensible answer is to sidestep the issue by disregarding the curricula needs of schools and to concentrate on what television is good at such as bringing into schools lively moving pictures of the kind that cannot be produced in any other way. Haigh's views are devoid of the considerations expressed earlier relating to the psychology of learning and educational television as they affect young children. Moreover, a series of programmes which does not fit into the curriculum could become an alternative curriculum and a situation arises whereby teacher and children are following two curricula (Choat 1982).

Macintyre (1981, 1983) reports on a three stage project in Scotland on the use of school broadcasting (radio and television) by primary and secondary school teachers. Stage 1 involved 100 primary and 100 secondary schools in an attempt to

YOUNG CHILDREN, TEACHERS AND EDUCATIONAL TELEVISION

identify factors which inhibit or encourage broadcast use and the awareness teachers have of what broadcasts are available. Stage 2 was intended to study the match between available broadcast materials and the school curriculum, and to select teachers and schools where apparently worthwhile use of broadcasting was being made. Stage 3 attempted to examine 24 primary schools and 18 secondary schools selected for good use of broadcasts, and further examine the context of this good use.

At each of the stages, teachers said they valued broadcasts highly as an important resource for teaching, as a motivator of pupils, and as a source of variety and stimulus. Decisions about broadcast use in primary schools were often based on timetabling rather than pedagogical considerations. Formal discussion of the curricular implications of the use of broadcasts was rarely found. Use in primary schools had a variety of functions. A broadcast sometimes served as a back-up to a centre of interest, or to reinforce a scheme of work in mathematics, or to act as the scheme of work in physical education or religious education or drama. Certain features of good use were assumed by the researchers: that teachers would prepare for using a broadcast by familiarizing themselves with the programme content and perhaps preparing relevant materials for the class; that the class would generally be prepared by the teacher; that pupils might be directed to carry out certain activities during a broadcast under the teacher's supervision; and that there would be some follow-up activity for most broadcasts either immediately or later or both. The Stage 3 teachers agreed with these interpretations of good use, and believed that a broadcast should be matched to the school curriculum and class work.

However, while some examples of good use were observed, it was rare to encounter a teacher who had thought about a broadcast and its relationship to the on-going work of the class and the needs of the pupils. Even among the good user primary school teachers, all of them used whole series sometimes and only about half made selections from series. Macintyre contends that in practice this means individual programmes are often quite unrelated to on-going work. Using broadcasts with a group of children taken from a class was rare. Indeed, Macintyre states, in their description of ideal use, primary teachers maintained that programmes should be taken "one class at a time". In fact, in 50% of

YOUNG CHILDREN, TEACHERS AND EDUCATIONAL TELEVISION

the schools, classes were joined for watching television. Only three quarters of the Stage 1 schools were equipped with colour television receivers, and comments about deficiencies of equipment and facilities were received from a third of the teachers. The most frequent comment was the wish for a video recorder and playback facilities. Apart from the more flexible timetabling offered by such a machine, the stop-start, review and preview facilities would be an educational advantage. None of the school buildings in Stage 3 was designed to facilitate use of broadcast materials and a variety of problems related to the siting of the television set were noted. The necessity to move classes some distance in order to view television was also an inhibiting factor. Nevertheless, Macintyre adds, conditions are rarely ideal in real school conditions but good use of broadcasts can be made in spite of that.

Although teachers are ultimately responsible for incorporating educational television into the curriculum, Choat, Griffin and Hobart (1984) assert that head teachers are not absolved from the considerations. The head teacher is responsible for running the school and for the curriculum. A few head teachers totally reject television and refuse to have a receiver in the school, while a small number are not enthusiastic and may restrict teachers' use or be content to rely on a monochrome (black and white) set. The purchase of a colour set is usually an indication of a head teacher's approval, but certain other factors need to be considered. The head teacher may remain in control and designate that teachers use certain series or restrict the teachers to one or sometimes two series each week. The head teacher could allow autonomous selection of series by teachers, but this might cause a problem. The booklets which accompany series have to be ordered early in the summer term for the series which begin in the following autumn term. The ordering is normally dealt with by the head teacher and she has the option of limiting the order to what she feels the staff may need. Acquisition of a video recorder also indicates a head teacher's acceptance of educational television. Many of these machines are purchased through fund raising activities or donations from parent/teacher associations. The head must agree with the purchase otherwise she would suggest alternative uses for the money. However, the main consideration revolves around how the head teacher evaluates educational

YOUNG CHILDREN, TEACHERS AND EDUCATIONAL TELEVISION

television in the construction of the curriculum, i.e. whether the medium plays a useful function in the children's activities. Some head teachers may argue that educational television is extraneous to curriculum considerations and a bonus for the hard pressed and hard worked teacher to use as a resource in addition to the school curriculum. This attitude evades the issue. The presence of a television receiver in a school implies acceptance of it as a possible means to generate motivation in children, and the purpose of the curriculum is to design provisions for children's education.

Owing to the shortage of evaluative research, there is scant information on how effectively teachers of young children are using educational television. Van Zon (1977) sent two questionnaires to 400 infants' school teachers in Holland, but these merely elicited teachers' opinions of educational television. Also using the questionnaire method, Ayres (1972) sampled 142 elementary school teachers in Tennessee, USA, on their attitudes towards educational television. The teachers regarded educational television as an aid to their teaching, did not consider it a threat to themselves, had not encountered substantial problems in their use of it, and were of the opinion that it was a real asset in the learning process. They specifically felt that children were interested in the programmes; that presenters can help improve children's attitudes and levels of attainment in certain subjects; and that the medium can provide uniform instruction.

In 1974 the Committee for Educational Broadcasting and Television of the Permanent Conference of the Ministers of Cultural Affairs compiled a list of about 50 evaluation studies which had been conducted in the Federal Republic of Germany and West Berlin. In only twelve of the studies were teachers asked by questionnaire how they rated the overal effectiveness of educational television programmes. Because of this, Tulodziecki (1977) summarized only a few of the studies and concluded that, in the opinion of the teachers, motivation, demonstration of problems, mediation of information and visualization were the main functions of educational television programmes, but the personal influence of the head teacher seemed to influence their utilization - particularly in small schools.

Choat (1982) questioned 427 infants' school teachers in 28 local education authorities in

YOUNG CHILDREN, TEACHERS AND EDUCATIONAL TELEVISION

England and Wales on their use of educational television. Language and general interest series were used extensively and mathematics series to a much less extent, but no substantive evidence emerged of these series being incorporated into the curriculum. A preparation - broadcast - follow up routine appeared to be the norm with the broadcast and teachers' booklets used for inspiration. Broadcasts did not seem to be used as a continuous teaching element to provide experiences beyond children's normal school activities. Programmes were used mainly as a substitute for real life experience, and for class viewing, rather than according to children's individual needs. Much faith was placed by the teachers in the future acquisition of video recorders.

By tape recording structured open-ended interviews, Hurst (1981) discussed the logic teachers attributed to their decision on whether or not to use certain educational television broadcasts with 50 primary and secondary school teachers in East Sussex and Sierra Leone. He concluded that teachers are apathetic to broadcasts but that the main disincentives were technical and concerned the intrinsic characteristics of the medium and the limitations in the classroom. The advantages are the provision of material which is stimulating and motivating, creating an interest in a topic through lively, entertaining and illuminating treatment. Hurst adds that unfortunately many producers use themselves as distant teachers and their programmes are didactic in conception. Children often find them boring and fidget, and teachers draw the appropriate conclusions.

Owing to the shortage of research, little is known about the extent that teachers of young children are incorporating educational television into the curriculum, and it is left to others to speculate about what is happening in classrooms. For instance, Fiddick (1978) alleges that there is more than a suspicion from the broadcasters' side that some teachers are simply using educational television for a quiet life. To the conscientious teacher this is an intolerable assertion and difficult to quantify but Fiddick contends that the evidence is sensed in the number of teachers who do not take the teachers' notes and who do not trouble to send in the report cards on programmes. In the same vein, Lawler (1979) maintains that most teachers still consider television in school as an exceptional aid rather than as an important element of their work. He suggests that since television requires so much attention through eye and ear, it cannot play a supplementary role in the classroom and inevitably tends to take over from the teacher.

The efforts of the School Broadcasting Council's Education Officers to improve the use of educational television is outlined by Sumner (1981) who has to admit that attempts to improve the classroom use of the medium have not been as effective as hoped in engaging teachers' active participation. Too many teachers are led by circumstances, or by erroneous belief, into hoping that the broadcasts will do the teaching for them. Dean (1981) suggests that teachers and children are influenced by broadcasting, and the power of this influence means that teachers and children come to school with ready-made assumptions and ideas which will affect what they take from educational television programmes. Associating broadcasting with popular entertainment means for some teachers that school broadcasting is seen as a non-essential which can be cut when the going gets rough, or the use of broadcasts may be seen by a teacher as a sign of weakness, a pandering to the need to entertain children to get them to learn. Dean further states that the way a teacher is motivated may affect the way she uses educational television, especially if those senior to her and professionally powerful in the influence they have, give her the impression that they value this kind of activity less than work which is more obviously teacher inspired. Referring to the situation in America, Finn (1980) considers television an enormously effective learning tool that is readily available for use. It makes use of visual and auditory perception; it employs movement, music, colour and repetition; it entertains and informs; it hides and reveals; it portrays the present, the past and the future; and it is even fun to watch. With credentials like these, Finn feels that every teacher in America should be integrating television into his or her curriculum, but this has not happened.

Not all of the comments on teachers and educational television are derisory, some complimentary accounts can be found. Scherer (1977) for instance, believes it is a mistake to think that educational television programmes are replacing the live performance of teachers in the classroom. She believes the medium is a supplementary resource, not unlike books in libraries, and just as necessary; it does what the creative and talented teacher cannot do. Hames (1973) takes a similar stance and believes that a good teacher could be even better with the aid of television. A mediocre teacher could be good. A poor teacher could be mediocre and "the clueless numbskull who should never have been released on the unsuspecting world" will by using television at least allow the children to escape from uninspiring frustrations to perhaps a period of enlightenment. Hames' assertion regards educational television as a direct teaching instrument and fails to take account of the role played by the teacher in learning with young children.

Sympathy with teachers in sorting out the complexities confronting them when selecting an educational television series is expressed by O'Brien (1978), but he also criticizes their use of the medium. Assuming that the problems of equipment, viewing facilities and accommodation are resolved, the teacher has to be aware of which programmes will meet her needs. She has to decide on which series to watch, estimate their potential and requisition the teachers' booklet some four or five months in advance. Many teachers claim these considerations pose so many problems that the incentive to use educational television is lost. They also complain of inadequate opportunities for pre-viewing, insufficient data on the aims of series, and the planners arbitrariness in determining the content and timing of programmes. O'Brien acknowledges that some of these grievances are justified, but contends that the BBC and ITV programme companies consider teachers' expectations of educational television to be too high. He does not define clearly whether this is his or the producers' view, but adds that the "switch-on-watch-discuss" approach is devoid of preliminary planning, selection or structuring and is still the technique adopted by many teachers who think they are educating their pupils but are simply containing and restraining them.

A presumption has existed that teachers will automatically adopt and adapt to using television (Choat 1982). Lambert (1975) contends that the under-use of broadcasts in schools can be attributed to the lack of adequate training in the use of educational television in the pre-service stage, while the Bullock Report (1975) believes that the young teacher should learn how the medium can be made to serve her purpose and this is why it is so important for the subject to be explored in initial and in-service training. According to Sumner (1981), BBC Education Officers were in the practice of making yearly visits to colleges to lecture students but this tended to reinforce the belief that the main purpose of broadcasts was to entertain. Current BBC policy is to encourage teacher training establishments to be self-sufficient in the education of student teachers in the use of broadcast resources. To this end, day or half-day sessions for the in-service education of lecturers have been held in a number of institutions. Moreover, the BBC (1981 p.6) claims a teacher must be presented with the opportunity for in-service education on a very substantial scale because she shares in the experience of an educational television broadcast. Added to this, six million copies of teachers' notes were sold in 1979/80 and, allowing for the fact that all of these may not be read from cover to cover, the BBC considers that the in-service potential is, again, substantial.

Until very recently nearly all primary schools viewed live television broadcasts but 42 per cent of primary schools had a video recorder by the summer of 1982 (Independent Television Companies Association 1983); doubling the number in the previous year. This proliferation may alleviate the concern expressed by Lawler (1979) of teachers making timetabling excuses for not taking programmes or of taking a very minor role while a broadcast is in progress. Furthermore, Scherer (1977) also suggests that with a video recorder it is no longer necessary for timetables to be matched with off-air broadcasts. Programmes can be taped and used to suit curriculum needs, instead of competing with the off-air schedule, and stored for later use.

Thus, as the ITCA (<u>loc cit</u>) contends, apart from allowing programmes to be fitted conventionally into the timetable, acquisition of a video recorder should have other advantages. Broadcast material is more readily accessible to more teachers and children in a school, the machine's replay facility and the use of the stop and pause control enables a detailed study of programme ideas and style of presentation thereby assisting teachers to preview and plan well in advance, to select programmes according to children's needs, to integrate broadcasts into the work of the school and select programme content for particular purposes and for particular groups of children. Without a video recorder a teacher's preparation for viewing depends largely on the synopses in programme booklets, but with a video recorder the teacher should be alerted to possible difficulties in the material and have

YOUNG CHILDREN, TEACHERS AND EDUCATIONAL TELEVISION

prior knowledge of the notions, information, vocabulary, attitudes and skills which will be required of the children. But the ITCA maintains, not everything watched needs class preparation and follow-up. There can and should be opportunity for a spontaneous sharing of programme experience and a video recording could be stored until such use is appropriate. Teachers can also use video as a means to evaluate children's responses particularly when they edit programmes by the simple expedient of showing only parts of a broadcast. Moreover, it is not beyond the bounds of some young children to operate the video recorder themselves and in doing so develop new insights and responses to programme material. This enables a child to stop a programme to carry out exercises, freeze-frame, rewind and generally use the material to suit his own needs rather than be subject to a fleeting experience in the company of a mass of other learners when viewing off-air (Hurst 1981).

Therefore, as Bates (1983, 1981) maintains, a learner cannot interrupt, interrogate, or ask for clarification when watching an off-air broadcast, but he has more control with recorded television. Bates suggests that the learner has the possibility of becoming much more independent as a learner, but this depends to some extent on the accessibility of video and play-back equipment. This point is also made by Choat (1982) who states that flexible use of a video recorder does not appear to be possible when a primary school has six or more classes. It does not seem to ease the problems of timetabling, clashes with playtime and more than one class viewing a broadcast. This is caused largely by the video recorder being in use for long periods to record programmes, thereby restricting the time available for playback. Apart from the obvious disadvantage, a further problem is created. Most series for young children are broadcast during the morning, and teachers prefer to follow-up immediately after a broadcast. Afternoons are not considered suitable as the children are less attentive, and the end of the day is devoted to story.

There seem to be many problems which need to be resolved before educational television can be used effectively with young children. Evaluation of the medium's efficacy in young children's learning has received scant attention, but the crucial element is the recognition of its feasibility by the teacher (Choat 1984). This implies that the main consideration revolves around how head teachers and teachers cater for educational television in the construction of the curriculum, i.e. the provisions made to recognise the role of the medium in children's learning (Choat, Griffin and Hobart, 1984). It was further indicated by Choat (1982, 1983b) that educational television was primarily used as a means to assist young children's language and mathematics, and as an inspiration for topic work. But are the series which teachers take provided for in the school's language and reading policies or are they irrelevant? If the latter is so, what is the justification for certain series being used? Similarly, a mathematics policy of individual learning may be decided upon or a mathematics scheme followed. How does educational television fit into either of these? Perhaps neither language nor mathematics series is thought appropriate and development in the disciplines is sought through general interest series. How does the curriculum enable this provision to be made? Centres of interest or topics are common features of education in the early years. How does educational television relate to them? Are there curriculum principles on what should be viewed by the children or does television regulate what is seen? These are some of the questions which are considered in later chapters.

REFERENCES

Amey, L.J. (1976), *Visual Literacy: Implications for the Production of Children's Television Programs*, Halifax, Nova Scotia. Dalhousie University School of Library Service.
Ayres, J.B (1972), *Elementary School Teachers' Attitudes Toward Instructional Television*, The Journal of Experimental Education, 41, pp. 1-4.
Bailey, K. (1973), *A Note on School Broadcasting*, in "Early Years at School", ed. Allen, D., London. BBC p.6.
Ball, S. and Bogatz, G.A. (1970), *The First Year of Sesame Street: An Evaluation*, Princeton, New Jersey. Educational Testing Service.
Bates, A.W. (1984), *Broadcasting in Education*, London. Constable.
Bates, A.W. (1983), *Adult Learning from Educational Television: The Open University Experience*, in "Learning from Television: Psychological and Educational Research", ed. Howe, M.J., London. Academic Press, pp. 57-77.
Bates, A.W. (1981), *Some Unique Educational*

Characteristics of Television and Some Implications for Teaching and Learning, Journal of Educational Television, 7, pp. 79-86.
BBC (1981), Broadcasts and Teacher Education, London. BBC Education.
Blenkin, G.M. and Kelly, V.A. (1981), The Primary Curriculum, London. Harper and Row.
Bliss, J., Goater, M., Jones, C. and Bates, A.W. (1983), Piaget's Theories and Some Possible Implications for Educational Television, Journal of Educational Television, 9, pp.33-46.
Bogatz, G.A. and Ball, S.J. (1971), The Second Year of Sesame Street: A Continuing Evaluation, Princeton, New Jersey. Educational Testing Service.
Bryant, J., Alexander, A.F. and Brown, D. (1983), Learning from Educational Television Programs, in "Learning from Television: Psychological and Educational Research", ed. Howe, M.J., London. Academic Press, pp. 1-30.
Calvert, S. and Watkins, B. (1979), Recall of Television Content as a Function of Content Type and Level of Production Feature Use, Paper presented in a symposium at the meeting of the Society for Research in Child Development, San Francisco. March.
Central Advisory Council for Education (England) (1967), Children and their Primary Schools (The Plowden Report), London. HMSO.
Choat, E. (1984), Pre-Operational Children and Educational Television, Journal of Educational Television, 10, pp. 151-156.
Choat, E. (1983a), A Strategy for Reviewing the Role of Educational Television in Infants' Schools, British Journal of Educational Technology, 14, pp. 127-136.
Choat, E. (1983b), Language, Mathematics and Educational Television in Infants' Schools, Journal of Educational Television, 9, pp.47-55.
Choat, E. (1982), Teachers' Use of Educational Television in Infants' Schools, Educational Studies, B. pp. 185-207.
Choat, E. (1981), Understanding in Young Children's Mathematics, Mathematics in School, 10, pp.18-21.
Choat, E. (1980), Mathematics and the Primary School Curriculum, Windsor. NFER.
Choat, E. Griffin, H. and Hobart, D. (1984), Head Teachers and Educational Television for Children up to Seven Years of Age, Head

Teachers Review, Spring, pp. 5-8.
Choat, E., Griffin, H., and Hobart, D. (1983), A Rival System, The Times Educational Supplement, 18th November, p. 38.
Collins, W.A., Wellman, H., Keniston, A.H. and Westby, S.D. (1978), Age-Related Aspects of Comprehension and Interference from a Televised Dramatic Narrative, Child Development, 49, pp. 389-399.
Committee of Inquiry into the Teaching of Mathematics in Schools (1982), Mathematics Counts (The Cockcroft Report), London. HMSO.
Cook, T.D. and Conner, R.F. (1976), The Educational Impact, Journal of Communication, 26, pp.156-164.
Corder-Bolz. C.R., (1980), Mediation: The Role of Significant Others, Journal of Communication, 30, pp. 106-118.
Corteen, R. (1977), Television and Reading Skills, Symposium presented at the meeting of the Canadian Psychological Association, Vancouver. June.
Dean, J. (1983), Organising Learning in the Primary School Classroom, London. Croom Helm.
Dean, J. (1981), School Broadcasting and the Professional Development of Teachers, in "Broadcasts and INSET", ed. Sumner, H. London: The Educational Broadcasting Councils for the United Kingdom, pp. 35-44.
Dearden, R.F. (1976), Problems in Primary Education, London. Routledge and Kegan Paul.
Debes, J.L. (1969), The Loom of Visual Literacy, Audio-Visual Instruction, 14, pp. 25-27.
Department of Education and Science (1978), Primary Education in England: A Survey by HM Inspectors of Schools (The Primary School Survey), London. HMSO.
Department of Education and Science (1982), Education 5 to 9: An Illustrative Survey of 80 First Schools in England, London. HMSO.
Department of Education and Science (1975), A Language for Life (The Bullock Report), London. HMSO.
Educational Broadcasting Council for the United Kingdom (1982), Surveys of Viewing and Listening in U.K. Schools: Annual Reports 1981-1982, London: BBC.
Essex County Council (1983), Topics and Centres of Interest in the Primary School, Chelmsford. Essex C.C.
Fiddick, P. (1978), The Power to Teach, The

Guardian, 1st June, p.11.
Finn, P. (1980), Developing Critical Television Skills, The Educational Forum, 44, pp. 473-482.
Fowles, B.R. and Horner, V.M. (1974), Visual Literacy: Some Lessons from Children's Television Workshop, New York. Children's Television Workshop.
Fowles, B.R. and Voyat, G. (1974), Piaget Meets Big Bird: Is TV a Passive Teacher?, Urban Review, 7, pp. 69-80.
Gadberry, S. (1980), Effects of Restricting First Graders T.V. Viewing on Leisure Time Use, IQ Change, and Cognitive Style, Journal of Applied Developmental Psychology, 1, pp. 45-57.
Goddard, N., Hannah, A. and Mitchell, P. (1972), Aspects of Infants' Education, London ILEA Television Service.
Haigh, G. (1983), End of an Era, The Times Educational Supplement, 1st April, p.41.
Hames, J. (1973) Television in Education, London IBA.
Hayter, C.G. (1974), Using Broadcasts in Schools, London. BBC/ITV.
Himmelweit, H.T., Oppenheim, A.N. and Vince, P. (1958), Television and the Child, London. Oxford University Press.
Home, A. (1983), Children's Television and its Responsibilities: The Producer's Point of View, in "Learning from Television: Psychological and Educational Research", ed. Howe, M.J., London Academic Press, pp. 193-201.
Hurst, P. (1981), The Utilization of Educational Broadcasts, Educational Broadcasting International, 14, pp. 104-107.
Independent Broadcasting Authority (1978), Learning Through Television, London. IBA.
Independent Television Companies Association (1983), The Use of Video Recorders in Schools, London ITCA.
Inner London Education Authority (1981), ILEA Statement on the Curriculum for Pupils Aged 5 to 16, London. ILEA.
Kerr, J.F. (1968), The Problem of Curriculum Reform, in "Changing the Curriculum", ed. Kerr, J.F., London. University of London Press pp. 13-38.
Kirby, N. (1981), Personal Values in Education, London. Harper and Row.
Lambert, J. (1975), The Bullock Report and Educational Broadcasting, Dudley Educational Journal, 2, pp. 14-25.
Lawler, L. (1979), Educational Television 21 Years

On, Visual Education, February, pp. 21-22.
Lawton, D. (1973), Social Change, Educational Theory and Curriculum Planning, London. University of London Press.
Lesser, G.S. (1972), Learning, Teaching and Television Production for Children: The Experience of Sesame Street, Harvard Educational Review, 42, pp. 232-272.
Levinsohn, F.H. (1977), Can Television be Used to Teach Essential Skills, School Review, 85, pp. 297-311.
McCreesh, J. and Maher, A. (1976), Pre-School Education: Objectives and Techniques, London. Ward Lock Educational.
Macintyre, A. (1983), The Use of School Broadcasting: Research Findings and Implications for Change, Programmed Learning and Educational Technology, 20, pp. 224-227.
Macintyre, A. et al. (1981), School Broadcasting in Scottish Schools, Glasgow. Jordanhill College of Education.
Morgan, M. (1980), Television Viewing and Reading: Does More Equal Better?, Journal of Communication, 30, pp. 159-165.
National Association of Head Teachers (1983), Language and the Primary School, Haywards Heath, NAHT.
Noble, G. (1975), Children in Front of the Small Screen, London. Constable.
Oakley, S. (1981), The Use of Educational Broadcasts in a Diploma Course, in "Broadcasts and INSET", ed. Sumner, H., London. Educational Broadcasting Councils for the UK, pp. 51-61.
O'Brien, T. (1978), Media Obstacles, The Times Educational Supplement, 15th September, p.28.
Pluckrose, H. (1979), Children and their Primary Schools, Harmondsworth. Penguin.
Report of the Committee on the Future of Broadcasting (1977), (The Annan Report), London. HMSO.
Robinson, K. (1981), Educational Broadcasts and the In-Service Education of Teachers, in "Broadcasts and INSET", ed. Sumner, H., London. Educational Broadcasting Council for the UK, pp. 45-50.
Salomon, G. (1979) The Interaction of Media, Cognition and Learning, London. Jossey-Bass.
Salomon, G. (1976), Sesame Street Around the World: Cognitive Skill Learning Across the Cultures, Journal of Communication, 26, pp. 138-144.
Salzberger-Wittenberg, I., Henry, G. and Osborne, E.

(1983), *The Emotional Experience of Learning and Teaching*, London. Routledge and Kegan Paul.

Scherer, M. (1977), *TV: The Classroom Co-Star*, School and Community, 63, pp. 24-26.

Sprigle, H.A. (1972), *Who Wants to Live on Sesame Street?*, Childhood Education, 49, pp. 159-165.

Sumner, H. (1981), *Introduction to "Broadcasts and Inset"*, ed. Sumner, H., London. Educational Broadcasting Council for the UK, pp. 5-14.

Thoules, R.H. (1969) *Map of Educational Research*, Windsor. NFER.

Tulodziecki, G. (1977), *Educational Television in the Federal Republic of Germany*, Programmed Learning and Educational Technology, 14, pp.108-116.

Van Hoose, J. (1978) *TV: The Effective Aide for Affective Education*, Phi Delta Kappa, 59, pp.674-675.

Van Zon, D. (1977) *Educational Television Programmes for Infants. The First Projects: Results of Research*, Programmed Learning and Educational Technology, 14, pp. 103-107.

Wade, B. and Poole, R.A. (1983), *Response to Educational Television: A Case Study*, Journal of Educational Television, 9, pp. 21-32.

Williams, T.M. (1981), *How and What do Children Learn from Television?*, Human Communication Research, 7, pp. 180-192.

CHAPTER TWO

HOW EVALUATION WAS CONDUCTED

The Incorporating Educational Television into the Curriculum for Children up to the Age of Seven Years Project (July, 1982 to August, 1985) was established to investigate teachers' attitudes to television in the classroom, to ascertain whether educational television programmes influenced teaching methods, and to indicate the extent that teachers recognised educational television as part of the normal curriculum or treated it as a separate entity.
   The lack of previous research into educational television and young children necessitated the first fourteen months being spent on devising means to carry out the full-scale enquiry. It was necessary to identify the range of programmes of interest and establish research procedures (Choat, Griffin and Hobart 1985). Thus, the project evolved into three phases, Phase I to conduct pilot work, Phase II to carry out the main survey and Phase III to analyse data and undertake a limited number of experiments and case studies.
   The pilot work indicated the need for constant contact with teachers throughout the research, that the method should be longitudinal, and that research could generate in-service education. The latter aspect was seriously considered. Some pilot study teachers expressed that they wanted to use educational television more effectively, and this warranted not only retaining the aspect but incorporating it within the main survey. Aligning in-service education with research produces an unusual methodology and it was essential to ensure that the in-service elements would not interfere with research issues. A procedure was resolved that enabled the two spheres to be combined but ensured that in the research findings bias was kept to a

HOW EVALUATION WAS CONDUCTED

minimum. The in-service element would not be dealt with until the relevant research had been completed. The final questionnaire on Curriculum and Learning was intended to discover whether the input received during the in-service sessions had created any change and to evaluate how teachers related educational television to the curriculum.

Figure 2.1 shows the stages and timing of the Phase II components. Each teacher was required to complete a pro forma on her intentions for one series she was going to use, fill-in a weekly checklist on her use of programmes and at the end of the term summarise whether her intentions had been fulfilled. It became evident during the pilot phase, and from visits to schools and classrooms, that language, mathematics and topic work were the range of programmes of interest. The weekly monitoring ceased at the end of the first term but questionnaires were designed to analyse the relationship teachers had between educational television and language, mathematics and topic work. Details and conclusions reached from these are reported in length by Choat, Griffin and Hobart (1987) but the features which have a bearing on teachers use of television are contained in Chapter 5. Very few nursery teachers participated in the pilot work and as this was likely also with the main study it was necessary to provide a means whereby their views could be obtained. A questionnaire was designed to be completed by an additional sample of nursery teachers. The in-service sessions also enabled the teachers' reactions to educational television to be gauged.

Each Local Education Authority in England and Wales was asked if they wished to participate in Phase II and eighteen accepted the invitation. These LEAs were requested to form groups of approximately twenty teachers around a nucleus of schools. This would have allowed the project team to make more visits to teachers and schools than if the teachers were recruited from individual schools. However, some Inspectors/Advisers wished to involved as many schools as possible and sometimes one or two teachers from different schools formed the groups. Therefore the groups varied in their composition but covered every region of England and Wales except the north-east region of England, with teachers from one hundred and forty three schools. One group did not materialize owing to local problems and this meant that seventeen groups (Appendix A), consisting of two hundred and fifty nine teachers, formed

HOW EVALUATION WAS CONDUCTED

Figure 2.1: <u>Plan of Phase II of the Project</u>

September, 1983 to August, 1984

	Teachers' Monitoring of a Series	Teachers' Attitudes to Curriculum Content	Nursery Survey	In-Service Sessions
TERM I	Intention with Series Weekly Check List for each Programme in the Series Summary of Term's Monitoring	Language Questionnaire		General Matters Relating to Educational Television Language
TERM II		General Interest Series Questionnaire Mathematics Questionnaire	Nursery Teachers' Questionnaire	Topic Work Mathematics
TERM III		Curriculum and Learning Questionnaire		Curriculum and Learning

HOW EVALUATION WAS CONDUCTED

the sample.
 Choat (1982) indicated that certain series were more popular than others, but group leaders were asked to arrange for an even distribution of the series monitored as far as this was possible. For example, when a teacher had decided to watch three series, one series might be common to most teachers but the other two series less popular. In these circumstances, it was helpful if the teacher monitored one of the less popular series. Trying to procure an even distribution was awkward as some series did not have very large audiences, and two series did not begin until Term II. Nevertheless, most group leaders managed to secure a reasonable distribution. It was stressed to the teachers that they should not watch and monitor programmes unrelated to their teaching. They were asked to act as they would normally and use a programme only when they felt it suitable to their needs. They were instructed to cease monitoring if they became disillusioned with a series and to give their reasons on the end of term pro forma. Some teachers did not monitor in Term I but in Term II when the two further series were broadcast, and three teachers who had monitored in Term I also monitored a second series. The series, their aims and intended age-ranges as described in the Annual Programme Guides, were:-

Language

 Let's Read...With Basil Brush (Central, an introduction to reading, 5-6 years); this series is not intended as a reading scheme off the air but as a support for teachers who require resources for language experience, early reading activities and stories to interest young children.
 Talkabout (BBC, early language, 5-7 years); the programmes present material in the form of stories, songs and games through which children may experience a variety of language use and style. In related activities they are encouraged to explore new ideas through their own words. This series is particularly useful to young children for whom English is a second language.
 Words and Pictures (BBC, early reading, 5-7 years); the series aims to encourage children in the early stages of reading through the enjoyment of shared stories, rhymes and reading practice. The programmes are intended to help young children to develop the skill of anticipation in reading for

HOW EVALUATION WAS CONDUCTED

meaning, encourage them to attend to the differences in letter forms and sounds, to concentrate on the consonants and blends in the initial position and use these as an aid to reading.

Look and Read (BBC, reading fluency, 7-9); this series is for children who have some reading ability but lack fluency or have learning gaps. Its first aim is to motivate them to read an exciting story. The second aim is to introduce a number of reading strategies which can be developed as an aid to reading the text. The programmes include work on sight vocabulary, phonic skills, language patterns and conventions, structure of words, context cues and comprehension at different levels. Children are encouraged to read direct from the screen during the programmes.

Mathematics

1..2..3..Go! (Central, an introduction to mathematics, 4-6 years); the eighteen programmes in this series are intended to supplement the early stages of learning about numbers together with ideas about time, money, length and simple shapes according to the needs of the children. Teachers should be able to incorporate the programmes into their own schemes of work.

Maths-in-a-Box (BBC, mathematics, 6-7 years); a mathematical adventure story in ten episodes that assumes some slight prior knowledge of mathematics, in particular experience of counting, number names and numerals up to nine and correct use of terms such as bigger, smaller, between, above, etc.

General Interest and Miscellany

You and Me (BBC, compendium, 4-5 years); a series transmitted four days each week for nursery and reception class children to enrich their language and mathematics and to stimulate their interests. The mathematical and reading elements are combined with books, rhymes, sketches and short films, and scenes with puppets explore areas of emotional development and imaginative games.

My World (Yorkshire, general interest, 4-6 years); twenty eight programmes for nursery and infants' school classes that offer experiences which will widen the children's understanding of the world in which they are growing up and of the relationships which they will face in and outside home. The material in each programme can be used as

HOW EVALUATION WAS CONDUCTED

a starting point to a variety of creative and written work.

<u>Alive and Kicking</u> (Central, all about me, 5-8 years); nine topics are explored in this series for and about infants. Each topic is treated in two programmes. The first programme features families with young children and is built around the children, their activities at school, home and at play with siblings, friends, parents and other adults in their lives. The second programme develops the theme through stories, poems, mime, drama, film, art, problem solving and games.

<u>Stop, Look, Listen</u> (Central, environmental studies/language development, 6 years and over); the series aims to provide a widening of experience, to help young children become more observant of sights and sounds, to make them more aware of the significance of everyday objects and events and to assist them to express themselves better in a range of media.

<u>Seeing and Doing</u> (Thames, miscellany, 6-7 years); a topic-based series which aims to provide stimulating activities and experiences for young children, with follow-up ideas for language/writing, science/number activities, music, drama and creativity. The programmes are intended as stepping-off points to be used in conjunction with support material, books, visual aids, visits, etc.

<u>Watch</u> (BBC, miscellany, 6-8 years); the series aims to widen the experience of young children and to stimulate their imagination.

1..2..3..Go! and Alive and Kicking both commenced in the Spring Term, but all the other series began in the Autumn Term. Talkabout and Maths-in-a-box (fortnightly) ceased at the end of the Spring Term but the remaining series continued throughout the Summer Term. In addition to these specific series for young children, some teachers used series which were intended for children beyond seven years of age.

No attempt was made to differentiate between the types of schools and areas in which the teachers in the sample were teaching. Furthermore, recruitment into nursery and infants' schools was minimal in the early eighties with most schools staffed mainly by teachers with at least six years experience. Nevertheless, it was necessary to determine the age-range taught by each teacher (Table 2.1). The distribution provided a representative sample for each age-range in spite of

HOW EVALUTION WAS CONDUCTED

Table 2.1: <u>Classes taught according to age-range of children</u>

	Age-range of classes					
	Below 5 yrs.	5-6 yrs.	4-6 yrs.	5-7 yrs.	6-7+ yrs.	Total
Number of teachers	30 (11.4%)	67 (25.6%)	33 (12.6%)	44 (16.8%)	88 (33.6%)	262 (100%)

a third of the teachers being responsible for top infants and a quarter for the reception class.

Although the teachers were encouraged to monitor less popular series to enable a cross-section of all the series being broadcast to be monitored, the distribution still favoured the more popular series. The situation was not helped by Alive and Kicking and 1..2..3..Go! commencing in Term II. Nevertheless, apart from Alive and Kicking and Let's Read with Basil Brush each other series was viewed by a sufficient number of teachers to give reliable conclusions (Table 2.2) Nevertheless, remarks appertaining to these two series are dealt with in the comments on general interest and language series respectively. The junior school series are similarly discussed within the subject to which they are appropriate.

The pilot work indicated that many teachers of young children followed a preparation-broadcast-follow-up routine, and did not regard an educational television programme as a supplement within their planned provisions. It was necessary therefore to investigate how programmes were treated by teachers, what ensued prior to a broadcast, what transpired during off-air transmissions and video playbacks and what happened when broadcasts had ended. Effective use of educational television has a prior requisite in the person of the teacher, how she incorporates the medium into the curriculum and how she abides by the psychology of learning to promote motivation and the fulfilment of children's needs and interests. As explained in Chapter 1, the preparation-broadcast-follow-up technique can lead to an over-emphasis of a programme and separate it from children's normal activities. Other activities may be abandoned in order to concentrate on a special display, etc., but when educational television is incorporated into the

HOW EVALUATION WAS CONDUCTED

curriculum preparation can be embedded in the children's activities prior to the broadcast, and follow-up absorbed in the continuation of these activities. Neither is it always necessary to follow-up with written work, art work and models. Children should be allowed to experience a situation practically, express their feelings through play, or merely observe a broadcast.

Along with classroom visits and in-service sessions, the weekly monitoring through the completion of checklists provided information on how the teachers were using television. As Figure 2.1 shows, the monitoring lasted for one term - a period of ten weeks during the autumn term. This term was selected as the teachers had not had time to be influenced by the in-service sessions and would reflect the practice carried out by the thousands of other teachers not participating in the project, i.e. the practice normally adopted by teachers of young children when using television. The pilot work had indicated that one term was sufficient for the teachers' activities with educational television to be assessed.

Three particular weeks were selected for sampling purposes, the third, sixth and ninth weeks. When a teacher did not use a broadcast on one of these weeks, an adjoining week's checklist was substituted for analysis. Each item on the checklist was analysed according to age-range taught and series monitored. Nevertheless, every checklist for each of the ten weeks of monitoring was scrutinised for further breakdown on individual series and for comments which related to individual items.

REFERENCES

Choat, E. (1982), <u>Teachers' Use of Educational Television in Infants' Schools</u>, Educational Studies, 8, pp. 185-207.

Choat, E., Griffin, H. and Hobart, D. (1985), <u>Investigating Educational Television and the Curriculum for Young Children: Some Pilot Phase Features</u>, British Journal of Educational Technology, 16, pp. 60-65.

Choat, E., Griffin, H. and Hobard, D. (1987), <u>Language, Mathematics, Topic Work and Television</u>, Beckenham, Croom Helm.

HOW EVALUATION WAS CONDUCTED

Table 2.2: The educational television series monitored by the teachers and the number of instances of use for language, mathematics and general interest

	Monitoring	Language	Questionnaires Mathematics	General Interest
Number of teachers who monitored	262			
Number of teachers in sample		227	193	184
Number of teachers who used educational television		206 (90.7%)	72 (37.3%)	155 (84.2%)
Language Series				
Words and Pictures	56	113	14	44
Let's Read with Basil Brush	5	13	-	3
Look and Read	11	25	2	14
Talkabout	29	54	3	29
Total	101	205	19	90
Mathematics Series				
1..2..3..Go!	9	12	25	8
Maths-in-a-Box	13	28	27	23
Junior School Series	1	-	-	-
Total	23	40	52	31

HOW EVALUATION WAS CONDUCTED

Table 2.2: The educational television series monitored by the teachers and the number of instances of use for language, mathematics and general interest (Continued)

	Monitoring		Questionnaires	
		Language	Mathematics	General Interest
General Interest Series				
Watch	48	92	18	86
Seeing and Doing	18	40	5	34
Alive and Kicking	4	4	1	19
Stop, Look, Listen	18	34	3	33
My World	16	27	2	18
You and Me	27	34	19	26
Junior School Series	-	1	-	1
Total	131	232	48	217
Other Junior School Series	7	-	-	-
Grand Total	262	477	119	338
Average number of series per teacher using them		2.3	1.7	2.2

CHAPTER THREE

TEACHERS USING TELEVISION

Very little would have been gained by continuing the monitoring for a longer period. Some checklist replies were beginning to be repetitious and the teachers had clearly indicated how they were using educational television. Furthermore, the teachers were to be asked to complete questionnaires on language, mathematics, topic work, the curriculum and learning, apart from attending in-service sessions.

Series Discontinued During Monitoring

Nine teachers discontinued using the series they were monitoring, and a further sixteen teachers ceased to use another eighteen non-monitored series. Although the teachers were asked to behave as they would normally, the in-service discussions indicated that a few teachers had continued to monitor because they were participating in the project whereas they would have abandoned a series in normal circumstances. Moreover, discontinuation cannot be gauged solely in terms of volume for this does not distinguish between incorrect choice by the teacher, dissatisfaction with presentation, content above or below the children's ability levels, and other possible reasons. In some instances a series may have been carrying out its aims but was not conducive to what a teacher required. This appeared to be the situation with Words and Pictures. The series was discontinued by five teachers because it was either too simple or too advanced for the children, but reference was made to phonics in this connection.

TEACHERS USING TELEVISION

Programmes Not Taken

Two hundred and twenty seven programmes were reported as not taken. This would have been greater if teachers who had discontinued series had sent in checklists for the weeks they had not viewed programmes. The responses were divided into four areas:-

- a) Seventy eight instances of programmes not being taken because of organisational difficulties.
- b) Forty six instances of time not being available because of other activities. This mainly occurred during the Christmas period when teachers found it difficult to fit in work not specifically connected with Christmas.
- c) Seventy six instances of teachers being absent or half-term coinciding with broadcasts, even when these had been repeated.
- d) Twenty seven instances of teachers deciding not to take a programme. They said it was unsuitable or did not fit in with the work the children were doing. Twenty of these instances were concerned with a Watch multi-ethnic unit. Sixteen teachers had watched these programmes and not found them suitable. This figure was far in excess of any other unit of programmes. Some effort should be made with programmes of this kind for teachers in areas which may or may not contain children of ethnic origin but it must be questioned whether the programmes were suitable for children up to seven years of age or whether a different approach was needed. However, there were some favourable comments on the programmes.

Approximately one programme per teacher was reported as not taken but this was not evenly distributed as was instanced by one teacher's viewing pattern:-

Week 1 : Television not working
Week 2 : Programme taken

TEACHERS USING TELEVISION

    Week 3 : Not in school for programme
    Week 4 : School activity made it impossible to view programme
    Week 5 : Working in classroom and forgot the time
    Week 6 : Programme taken
    Week 7 : Programme taken
    Week 8 : Television room being used by someone else
    Week 9 : Programme taken by another teacher who said it was not very good and no follow-up work done
    Week 10: No response

Selection and Published Material

Both the BBC and ITV companies publish annual programme booklets at the end of the spring term. These booklets provide information about all of the educational television series to be transmitted in the following school year. Details of individual series are given with the days and times of transmissions, and the age range for which each series is intended. The aims of the series are normally given along with descriptions of the programmes. For example, the IBA booklet for 1983/84 stated that My World in the autumn term would consist of ten new programmes which examined family and social relationships young children might experience. The first five programmes were concerned with the closest relationships; the child, parents, brothers and sisters, grandparents and neighbours. The five programmes in the second half of term looked at the child's immediate environment and offered an opportunity to understand that in our multi-cultural society children are brought up in a great variety of environments. On the other hand, Stop, Look, Listen, Talkabout, Maths-in-a-Box and Watch listed only the title for each week's programme. The annual programme booklets therefore gave the teachers an opportunity to judge which series were suitable for the class they were taking in the following September.

The BBC and ITV companies also published teachers' booklets to accompany each series, and issued further support material for certain series. The teachers' booklets varied in their presentation, but the intention was to support teachers in their use of educational television. Each programme in a series was set out separately and matters relating to it were explained. A brief description of the

TEACHERS USING TELEVISION

programme content was usually included and some booklets offered advice on preparation. For example, notes on the Asian Wedding programme in Watch suggested bringing in some wedding photographs and discussing weddings in general, talking about lucky charms, and pointing out that rice and confetti are thrown at the couple to bring them luck at British weddings, but at Hindu weddings the bridal pair are given a coconut. For the Harvest programme in Seeing and Doing the teacher was advised to discuss the meaning of harvest and why it is celebrated, to collect pictures of different kinds of crops, to try out at home a simple recipe for making bread before attempting the activity with children, to practice the song "Oats and Beans and Barley Grow" with actions and to look up the apple-picking poem contained in the anthology.

Some booklets, particularly those for Stop, Look, Listen, Words and Pictures, Seeing and Doing, Watch and Talkabout, contained book lists from which a teacher might have supplemented programme content after a broadcast. Much in the booklets was devoted to suggestions for follow-up activities. My World and Seeing and Doing specified language, mathematics, science, art and craft, and gave ideas on how each subject could have been pursued after the programmes. Watch included innumerable exercises and activities for the children to undertake, as did Words and Pictures - together with its worksheet for each programme. Look and Read, was primarily a junior school series and the booklet insisted that children would benefit more from the series unless adequate time was given to follow-up work. A section featuring activities useful to children for whom English was a second language was contained for each programme but language and reading activities which emphasised phonics, morphemic structure, language patterns and language conventions were stressed. A set of spirit duplicating masters of illustrated worksheets which offered a wide variety of reading and writing activities that include crosswords, cloze passages, riddles on plot words, comprehension and language practice were available for purchase. The booklet stated, "the worksheets are an opportunity to reinforce many of the teaching points in the series, using the pupil's pamphlets as the source material". Both Maths-in-a-Box and 1..2..3..Go! provided many follow-up suggestions in mathematics. You and Me was the exception in the type of support material which it provided. It published a You and Me Book, costing £2.75, which went with the full year's broadcasts and took up items, stories and rhymes from the series but did not provide material linked to each programme. Typescript teachers' notes which listed the programmes and gave a brief outline of their content and a few follow-up suggestions were available. These notes were formerly free to teachers, but now each term's notes cost 25p.

Although the information in the booklets was a further source for a teacher to select which series to use, there were certain restrictions. The BBC encouraged teachers to order booklets early, and in 1983/84 gave a 7 1/2% discount on orders received by 17th June. Early ordering meant early delivery since publications were despatched to schools in the sequence in which they arrived. Late orders were not always supplied since print runs were limited to expected sales. Orders received after 8th July were not guaranteed to be met. The ITV companies required order forms to be returned by the 1st May and warned that orders received after that date might not have been fulfilled. However, they stated that booklets were usually available throughout the school year but late orders had to be accompanied by a cheque or postal order for the appropriate amount.

Added to the necessity to order well in advance, the improbability of securing booklets after the specified dates could cause annoyance for some teachers. If they change their teaching plans or are given an alternative class to what was originally intended and consequently decide to take a different series it is unlikely that they will secure a teachers' booklet for their new choice. Similarly, if a teacher receives the booklet for her chosen series, discovers it is not what she anticipated and decides to abandon it, then there is not much hope of securing a booklet for the alternative series. At the in-service sessions, some teachers expressed annoyance with the early ordering, and uncertainty of securing booklets if the order were missed. However, most teachers did not find the ordering restrictions a disadvantage.

Two thirds of the teachers found the annual programme booklets/teachers booklets useful in helping them to decide on which series to use but the percentage for general interest series, seventy two per cent, was considerably higher than for language series, fifty five per cent. The annual programme booklet's usefulness for general interest series was attributed to listing the themes covered throughout the year, but the general interest series teachers' booklets seem to influence selection more than the annual programme booklets. Ideas for preparation and follow-up work featured prominently in the teachers' remarks on general interest and language series booklets.

Sixty five per cent of the teachers taking mathematics series found the published material helpful but more were influenced by the teachers' booklet rather than the annual programme booklet in their choice of series. Follow-up activities in the booklets was again the main reason.

The published material had no effect on eighteen per cent of the teachers who had decided to use a series irrespective of what it declared (particularly with language and general interest series). They had used the series previously and based their decision on that experience.

Background Information

For each of the three weeks sampled, four fifths of the teachers maintained that the teachers' booklets were useful in supplying background information. There were however variations with age-groups and series. Teachers of the higher age-ranges made more use of the booklets than those of the lower age-ranges but use of the Talkabout booklet for background information increased by the ninth week as did use of the Seeing and Doing booklet for the sixth and ninth weeks. The Maths-in-a-Box booklet was used by every teacher on two of the three sample occasions, while the booklet for 1..2..3..Go! was used by only just over half of the teachers. It was felt that the booklet was unnecessary as the 1..2..3..Go! programmes were used as revision of what the children had learned in the first term.

The format of the You and Me material was explained previously and this came in for criticism by teachers who did not use it for background information. It was said to be very limited and muddled. The teachers would have liked more details on programmes to assist them with their planning. However, there were other teachers who felt a booklet was unnecessary for the younger children as they had no intention of following-up with systematized work. Stop, Look, Listen was another topic series booklet that was accused of having insufficient detail, lacking in ideas and scanty information. The My World booklet also came in for criticism for lack of detail and information and for giving notes purely on the format of programmes. Three teachers did not use the Watch booklet because programmes had been seen before and the story was well known. Non-usage of the Seeing and Doing booklet provided different emphases than those given for the other topic series. There were contentions that the material was of limited use and the ideas vague. A half of the teachers using the series did not feel a booklet was necessary for Talkabout; otherwise criticisms accused the booklet of containing details of the song and story but lacking detail on other features of programmes. That the ideas in the Words and Pictures booklet could have been more imaginative and did not inspire teachers was a common complaint. Unavailability of the booklets was the only explanation for not using the Look and Read material. Whether this was because they were not ordered or whether they had failed to arrive from the BBC was not made clear.

Preparing the Children

Approximately three quarters of the teachers stated that they found the booklets useful to prepare the children before broadcasts although the number had dropped slightly by the end of the term. The most noticeable declines were for Words and Pictures and My World, and these were confirmed by a similar drop by the teachers of the four to six and five to six-year-old age-ranges; the age-ranges for which the series were most popular. Apart from a gradual decline throughout the term by the teachers of the five to seven-year-old age-range the other age-ranges and series remained constant.

Various reasons were given for not using the booklets for preparation. These differed between the booklets being irrelevant, insufficient and not needed. Talkabout and Words and Pictures were the series for which least need was felt. The teachers preferred the children to watch programmes without preparation as they wished the story to be heard before discussing it or the story was taken for enjoyment only.

The You and Me material came in for further criticism. It was accused of being specifically geared for teacher/adult benefit and not for preparing the children. There was insufficient information to indicate what was going to happen in a broadcast and the booklet lacked details to assist with planning. On the other hand, it was also asserted that there was no need to prepare the children for a You and Me programme. The comments relating to the other general interest series for the younger children, My World, alleged that no details were given on preparing the children. The teachers who did not use the Watch and Seeing and Doing booklets declared that preparation was not necessary for the series. The Stop, Look, Listen booklet was considered unsuitable for preparation on account of its material being sparse and the real value of the programmes coming after broadcasts when the sequence of events and the 'why' could be discussed. Those teachers who did not prepare the children for mathematics broadcasts considered the procedure unnecessary. They did not want to spoil the surprise for the children, or preferred to just let the child watch to see if they enjoyed the programme or felt the children needed the stimulation of the programme beforehand. No direct reasons for lack of preparation were attributed to the teachers' booklets.

Making Materials

Half of the teachers claimed that they found the teachers' booklets useful for enabling them to make materials prior to broadcasts. Least use was made by the nursery teachers and, although very little material was made to use with You and Me, not a great deal was prepared for 1..2..3..Go! in the third week but the amount did increase gradually throughout the term. Stop, Look, Listen was another series for which the booklet was little used to help with material preparation. This might be because most programmes in the series were environmentally based and the teachers felt that very little could have been done to assist children with this. On the other hand, the Look and Read and Watch booklets were used extensively. The teachers using mathematics series insisted that they had a large selection of apparatus already in the classroom, and had no need to prepare more material. There were many assertions that no material was necessary for the language series and, for all of the series, some teachers wanted to watch the programmes first and make material afterwards, but there were other reasons such as 'no time' and 'no need' and 'follow-up not intended'.

Viewing Organisation

Most nursery and infants' teachers would accept

that each child in their class should be treated as an individual. This does not specify that all of their teaching is on an individual basis. It merely implies that each child should be recognised and treated as an individual with activities and work provided at his level of development and at his pace of learning. Obviously, there will be many occasions when certain children are dealt with on a one-to-one basis, but there are many other occasions when group work will feature as a provision. Apart from allowing children of similar ability to work together, groups also provide opportunities for children of different abilities to mix socially. There are instances too when a teacher feels it is necessary for children to be assembled as a class. This may occur for story, drama, movement, etc. when the teacher wishes all of the children to share in the experience or thinks that the activity is conducive for all of them to participate.

The organisation of children to watch educational television should not be distinguished from other organisational considerations. Some programmes might be ideal for class viewing as they are pertinent to all the children, particularly if connected with a topic the class are pursuing. The broadcast however must be such that it is at a level for each child to be able to take from it what is relevant to him. This does not suggest that children should be expected to abstract from the programme but that the teacher interprets the broadcast at levels appropriate to all of the children. In other words, although all of the children are watching the broadcast together, the teacher knows the children sufficiently well to interpret the programme for each child individually. This is made simpler when broadcasts are incorporated within the curriculum and are not regarded as a separate entity by emphasis on preparation, broadcast and follow-up.

There are instances however when class viewing is not desirable. These are more likely to occur with language and mathematics programmes when children are at various levels of development. It is appropriate in these circumstances for children of similar ability, for whom the programme is relevant, to watch in small groups. This is when the video recorder displays one of its useful functions. The programme can be recorded and shown only to the group concerned. Although it is feasible for a small group of children to watch an off-air transmission, this is not always possible because of the time of the broadcast and the siting of the television receiver in someone else's classroom or the hall. Small group viewing is more feasible with a video recorder when the remaining children have been assigned to other tasks or activities. A video recorder also enables individual viewing when an extract is required for a particular child or when a child himself wishes to playback something about which he is unclear or on which he needs reassurance.

Table 3.1: <u>Organisation of children's viewing according to number of teachers</u>

Type of series	Whole class	Small group	More than one class	No response
Language series	42	3	55	1
Mathematics series	18	2	3	-
General Interest series	94	5	30	2
All series	154	10	88	3

Only ten out of the two hundred and fifty five teachers who used language, mathematics and general interest series implemented small group viewing (Table 3.1). Four of these teachers used You and Me. One was a nursery teacher who allowed those children who wanted to watch to do so. The other three teachers had reception children and only those children to whom programmes were relevant watched them. Two teachers in team teaching situations withdrew small groups for viewing. One of these teachers had a group of top infants watching a video playback of Maths-in-a-Box when other maths groups were working with the other team member. In the other instance, only the reception children watched Talkabout on video. One teacher used video playback for a small group of older children to see Seeing and Doing. A further teacher also used the video to play back Maths-in-a-Box with a small group. The two remaining examples were with off-air broadcasts of Words and Pictures. One teacher restricted the series to less able six to seven-year-olds and the other teacher to the capable children in a reception class. Thus, four teachers used the video recorder and six teachers off-air broadcasts with small groups.

Whole class viewing was common with mathematics series irrespective of mixed age-ranges and children of different mathematical abilities. Organisation problems appeared to be the main reason for class viewing while it was also contended that there was no-one available to supervise the other children if just a small group watched television.

General interest series were normally treated as occasions when all of the class viewed together. The teachers felt that if all of the children viewed it enabled them all to contribute to class discussions and to exchange ideas. Class viewing was also regarded as a base for topic work and enabled preparation and follow-up to be undertaken with the whole class. It was explained that the interest level applied to the whole age-range and it was possible to develop themes to a greater or lesser extent with all of the children. Some teachers welcomed the video recorder to facilitate class viewing. They maintained that a video enabled them to watch without other classes being present and that a class of thirty children were able to concentrate better than a large group of sixty plus. There were several contentions that the television was timetabled for a certain time and no spare staff were available to be responsible for the remaining children if the class were split.

A lower percentage of teachers adopted class viewing for language series than for mathematics or general interest series. These teachers felt the whole class would benefit. Compared to mathematics and general interest series, the teachers did not feel they had to justify the whole class viewing.

However, although the percentage of children watching language series as a class was low it was high for mass viewing. A third of the entire sample joined with at least another class for watching educational television, but this embraced over a half for language series compared to a fifth for general interest series and just over a tenth for mathematics. The viewing groups ranged from approximately forty to sixty children but in some instances the figure increased to eighty or more children. Vertically grouped classes were joined to watch Words and Pictures, and in one instance three classes viewed the series together. Similarly three reception classes were joined to watch Talkabout. The school had two aerial points - the hall and a small quiet room but timetabling made this large group necessary.

Timetabling was mentioned by several teachers as the reason for mass viewing language series. For example, one school had one television set between six classes. Two middle infants' classes watched Words and Pictures on Mondays because the hall was free and there was ample room to watch together. The hall was being used for P.E. when the programme was repeated on Wednesdays. Timetabling of the resources room where the television was situated also caused problems. This was instanced in a school with a video recorder, but as the teacher took two other series, the third series, Words and Pictures, had to be shared with another class. The use of the hall was the main timetabling problem. It was used for assembly, P.E., movement, dance, singing, etc. and when the aerial point was situated there television had to be fitted in with these other activities but there were other reasons. The whole group was often timetabled for a language series when team teaching was in operation. A group of over seventy children viewed together because there was a large colour television in a room that accommodated that number. Timetabling, the use of the hall or a large room did not account for all the reasons. Large group viewing was justified because the programme was appropriate to all the children's needs. In other instances classes watched together because another series which the children viewed was broadcast on the same day and the teachers wished to separate the series by watching on different days.

Although fewer in number, the reasons offered for more than one class viewing mathematics and general interest series were similar to those for language. Timetabling difficulties in a large school, even with a video recorder, were common for general interest series. Three instances of over a hundred and twenty children watching a broadcast were given. It was said that Watch was viewed on Wednesdays by a large group because the Monday broadcast clashed with school prayers. It was further claimed that teachers in a school are given the chance to discuss the same programme when classes watch together. Teachers also mentioned that mass viewing was necessary because schools did not have enough television sets and even the acquisition of a video recorder did not seem to alleviate the problem.

The Independent Television Companies Association claimed that 42 per cent of primary schools had a video recorder by the summer of 1982 (see Chapter 1). Possession of a video recorder should offer flexibility in a teacher's use of educational television material to enhance the potential for children's learning. The teacher has greater control of what is presented than she has with an off-air transmission. The learner too has greater independence when extracts suitable to him are selected, or when a small group of children watch an extract that is relevant to an activity with which they are involved. Some capable infants' school children may even be able to operate the video recorder themselves to playback certain parts of a recording they wish to see again, use for their work, etc.

The top right-hand corner of each checklist indicated whether facilities were available for video recorder use in the teachers' schools. This was possible for thirty one per cent of the teachers on each of the three selected broadcasts. However, video use was not the regular practice for all of these teachers. Some varied between using off-air broadcasts and video recordings. There was little variation in the use of video recorders throughout the age-ranges, although teachers of the youngest children (below five, and four to six-year-olds) made slightly less use of the facility than the teachers of other age-groups. This drop was also reflected with the series. On each of the three sampled occasions, You and Me, was watched on video by only fifteen per cent of the classes compared to an average twenty per cent for all series.

Certain features associated with the availability and feasibility of the video recorder were mentioned previously and these re-occurred during discussions at the in-service sessions. Video recorder use rarely differed from treatment of an off-air broadcast. In the majority of cases, a programme was played through from beginning to end without interruption. Only in rare instances was the playback stopped for children's comments or for the teacher to explain what was depicted in the programme. The majority of teachers admitted that they rarely had the opportunity to preview recordings prior to playing them back with the children. On the whole, the video recorder was used to playback a recording to the children when it suited the teacher or when the viewing area was free.

There were some exceptions to the general pattern but only a few teachers stated that they used the stop-start controls. Three of these were observed taking a lesson and even such a small number demonstrated how effective this type of teaching can be. At one of the in-service sessions, a teacher explained how she pre-viewed each mathematics programme and used only those sequences which she felt were relevant to the children. Some teachers in another group saw the advantage of recording programmes and fitting them into their teaching, and indicated they would try this during the next school year. It was surprising that none of these teachers had considered this previously even though they had possessed video recorders for at least five years. Consequently, as there was little variation between off-air broadcasts and video recorded programmes, no attempt was made in the survey to distinguish how programmes were used by the two means.

Activities after programmes

Ninety per cent (third programme), eighty six per cent (sixth programme) and eighty five per cent (ninth programme) of the teachers indicated that they used programme material for further activities with the children. There were no significant differences in either age-ranges or series.

Lack of time, other commitments and pressure of other classroom activites were frequently quoted as reasons for not carrying out activities. The reasons applied to mathematics, language and general interest series but there were some exceptions for some series. For example, Maths-in-a-Box did not seem to inspire some teachers to want to undertake related activities. Words and Pictures programme content occasionally did not fit in with the general scheme of work so nothing was done. Two programmes in Talkabout, Who's Calling and The Foolish Tortoise were not pursued by some teachers because the children had no interest in them.

Compared to other units, the number of instances when programmes were not pursued rose steeply for the Watch multi-ethnic unit. Some teachers alleged that the children did not take to the programmes and lost interest, but on the whole the teachers said they were involved with another topic, felt the children would not benefit, considered the curriculum so full that there was little time left for work on Hindu customs and that the programmes were used for enjoyment and interest only because children of other cultures did not attend the school. On the other hand, the Nativity programmes appeared to create many opportunities for further activity.

Unsuitability of programme content was an additional reason for not pursuing further activities with other general interest series. There were several assertions that the Bells programme in Seeing and Doing was too technical with the children losing interest, the Migration programme did not provide relevant material to pursue and even the Fire and Harvest programmes failed to inspire further work. Similarly, the Ambulance, Hospital, Coalminer and Steel Band programmes in Stop, Look, Listen were thought to provide insufficient material to follow-up directly from the programme material. However, many teachers took this series out of interest and had no intention of continuing with activities because they were following a different topic. There were indications that My World was treated as an interest series and not pursued because it had no connection with classwork, although Shopping Trip and Playtime were criticised as inappropriate for four and five-year-olds. The main reason not to follow-on from You and Me appeared to be that the programme did not fit in with on-going activities.

Forms of activity

The activities undertaken primarily consisted of discussion, written work (including mathematics) and art or craft activities. In some instances only one activity was pursued but with others this evolved into two, three or sometimes four or more activities. General discussion amounted to the most popular form of activity irrespective of the series or age-range. It was usually conducted by the teacher with the children gathered around her by sitting on the floor or in the carpeted area of the classroom. On most occasions, the teacher went through the content of the programme reminding the children about what had occurred, asking them questions and inviting comments. Sometimes this was the total involvement but in other instances words had been prepared on the blackboard and the children were required to write about the theme or fill in the accompanying workbook or worksheet after the discussion. The teacher re-reading or re-telling the story in a programme was another popular way in which discussion was created. The manner in which it was approached did not differ drastically from ordinary story telling except that the teacher made occasional references to incidents in the broadcast. The children reacted very much as they would at ordinary story-telling time.

Some variations on the normal discussion patterns were witnessed during classroom visits. These usually occurred when the teacher did not make any direct reference to the actual broadcast but attempted to encourage the children to talk about their own experiences on the programme's theme. Discussion was also approached in a different way when items were placed around the classroom and the children encouraged to discuss these between themselves. Although class discussions were the norm, at one in-service group a teacher went to great length to explain that she considered discussion to involve one-to-one conversation between the teacher and the child and this was her way of treating a broadcast. It should be pointed out however that this teacher had a video recorder and used it to playback specific sequences with individual children, a very rare occurrence.

Overall, general discussion was pursued by over four fifths of the teachers. The only noticeable exceptions were the third week for 1..2..3..Go!, ninth week for Maths-in-a-Box, sixth week for Watch, and ninth week for Look and Read. This reaction to Look and Read was interesting as every teacher using the programmes had followed-up with discussion for the third and sixth weeks. Talkabout was another series that was used extensively for discussion.

Written work, which included recording mathematics, was another popular activity with roughly half the teachers following the practice. Percentage wise it was lower than discussion and more popular with teachers of the older children but nearly a fifth of the teachers with children below the age of five years required the children to do some written work. This was confirmed by the fact that thirty per cent of the teachers using You and Me required written work for the third week, and although the percentage declined for the sixth and ninth weeks, it was compensated by an increase in 1..2..3..Go! for those weeks. Written work associated with the Robinson Crusoe sequence of Watch was high, but not for the multi ethnic unit. As with discussion and art and craft activities, written work connected with Fire, broadcast by Seeing and Doing, rose markedly. This was probably due to the programme preceding Guy Fawkes Day. The written work for the general interest series usually consisted of writing about events in the programme or a connected theme introduced by the teacher.

The language series were treated similarly to the general interest series. Even with Talkabout, primarily an oracy series, half of the teachers taking the series required written work from the children. Look and Read was followed up with written exercises or recapitulation of the story episode. No instances were given of the project on houses, outlined in the teachers' booklet being followed. The written work following Words and Pictures frequently consisted of formation of the letter drawn in the programme by the magic pencil, sometimes writing about the story in the programme or filling in the worksheets copied from the teachers' booklet. It is interesting to note that the teachers' booklet made suggestions for things to talk about, things to make, things to do, and games to make and play but did not include ideas for writing. The worksheet, which regulated what each child watching the programme should write, was relied upon for this.

The amount of written work for 1..2..3..Go! rose sharply after the third programme. This consisted of children drawing sets and writing the numerical equation underneath, simply writing number statements and practising the writing of numerals. The latter aspect is interesting as the teachers' booklet gave many examples of practical activities and did not introduce the writing of numerals until the sixth week, the week when written work doubled that of previous weeks. The Maths-in-a-Box teachers' booklet abounded with suggested practical activities but the teachers pursued written work related or associated with number by extracting one of the suggestions which was not practical, i.e. 'on duplicated sheets prepared by the teacher, children map sets of animals on to their number properties'.

The occasions when art or craft activities were used was less than those for discussion and written work. Drawing and colouring a picture of an event or character from a programme was the most common practice. The teacher drew the picture in stages and the whole class followed her example or the children drew and coloured what they wished. Usually the picture had a sentence attached to explain what was represented. Another popular form of activity was a class frieze of a programme or for the topic associated with a number of programmes. Each child painted a certain aspect and this was added to the frieze.

TEACHERS USING TELEVISION

Models were not so much in evidence, but when they were they exhibited enterprise from the teacher. For example, one teacher, seizing on the possibilities offered by Robinson Crusoe in building his own house, encouraged the children to build models of their own houses at home, and then bring the models to school. This obviously involved parents who did part of the modelling in some cases, but a variety of models appeared. This gave the opportunity to introduce length by estimating size, defining shape, referring to symmetry, pointing out aspects of transformation, etc. Although the four programmes on Robinson Crusoe provided an opportunity to combine the unit with Look and Read, no evidence was produced that indicated a teacher had followed such a course. Nevertheless, art or craft activities were pursued more with the older age groups and series than those for the younger children. This was particularly so for Words and Pictures, although the percentage fell for the sixth and ninth weeks, and the 'Fire' programme in Seeing and Doing. Stop, Look, Listen however had a low response. The language series encouraged slightly less art and craft activity than the general interest series and the mathematics series showed a marked variation. A gradual increase was indicated for 1..2..3..Go!, but a decrease occurred for Maths-in-a-Box. This was accounted for by the accompanying increase in written work for 1..2..3..Go! when recording by drawing and colouring sets became the practice in a number of classes, and the transfer from sets to formally recording number equations with Maths-in-a-Box.

The teachers were asked whether they pursued any other activities apart from the categories listed. Many additional pursuits were given but the responses were in excess as many teachers listed activities which in fact should have been in the previous three categories. In some cases more than one activity was mentioned but the number of activities for the ten weeks of monitoring was collated (Table 3.2). Most categories in the table are self-evident but explanation of the column marked children's interest is necessary. Included in this classification are a wide variety of categories which were difficult to assign in other ways, i.e. making butter and cheese, teddy bears' picnic, Hallowe'en party, listening walk, class assembly, road safety, different types of collections brought from home, etc. Religious education could have been greater if assembly and work connected with

Table 3.2: The number of occasions other activities were pursued after programmes

Series	Music	Drama	Hand-writing	Play	R.E.	Making Games	Dance and P.E.	Children's Interests	Total
You and Me	10	5	1	15	–	3	3	5	42
Talkabout	18	14	–	–	–	3	3	13	51
Words and Pictures	35	15	9	2	–	2	10	11	84
Look and Read	–	1	–	–	–	–	–	1	2
Stop, Look, Listen	8	5	–	1	–	–	–	9	23
Seeing and Doing	12	3	–	–	3	–	–	13	36
Watch	8	23	–	1	1	1	5	54	90
My World	1	6	–	8	–	–	2	10	27
1..2..3..Go!	14	–	–	–	–	–	2	–	14
Maths-in-a-Box	4	–	–	–	–	–	–	2	6
Let's Read with Basil Brush	–	1	–	–	–	–	1	–	2
Alive and Kicking	–	–	–	–	1	1	2	4	8
Junior Series	10	2	1	1	–	–	3	3	20
Total	120	75	11	28	5	10	31	125	405

TEACHERS USING TELEVISION

Christmas had been included.
   Apart from the various activities included in children's interests, music and drama were the most favoured forms of other activity. The musical element arose mainly from the songs in Words and Pictures, Talkabout, and 1..2..3..Go! when the words and music appeared in the teachers' booklet but, there was little support for the Robinson Crusoe and Diwali songs from the Watch booklet. Drama was inspired by Talkabout, Words and Pictures and Watch, particularly with Robinson Crusoe in the latter series. In proportion to the number of teachers who monitored the series, Watch also provided more activities relating to children's interests than any other series. Nevertheless, the teachers' booklets for general interest series listed numerous suggestions for follow-up activities after programmes and, in proportion to the number of teachers taking the programmes over ten weeks, the amount of participation was low.
   Similarly, very few games were made to play, although a number of ideas were given in the Talkabout and Words and Pictures booklets. Dance and P.E. had minimal response, and it is interesting to note that only two teachers used the ethnic unit in Watch for this even though one programme was devoted to Indian Dancing. The lack of play inspired by the programmes was noticeable. My World is a series for four to six-year-olds but only one teacher throughout the ten broadcasts used a programme to encourage play. This might be attributed to the fact that the teachers' booklet was devoted to follow-up activities in formal subjects. More teachers used You and Me for play purposes, but again the percentage was low when compared to the number of teachers using the series. Reference was made earlier to the teachers' contentions of the inadequacy of the support material for this series but the brief notes did state that 'children learn a tremendous amount about the world before they start 'proper' school, and they do ths chiefly by talk, <u>play</u> and stories'. However, the limited number of suggested follow-up activities contained very few play activities. Most were structured activities whereby the children follow instructions given by the teacher.
   It is not surprising that follow-up in the majority of cases was a structured exercise directly related to the programme. Most of the teachers' booklets emphasised follow-up with a set of prescribed subject activities, and play was rarely

TEACHERS USING TELEVISION

Figure 3.1: **Introductory remarks and terms used in the teachers' booklets relating to follow-up and associated activities**

Series	Teachers' Booklet Comments
You and Me	Talk about (a few topics). Follow-up (a few suggestions for early reading; early mathematics).
Talkabout	Programme follow-up – Using the television broadcast as a starting point, teachers could introduce some of the activities suggested in the notes for each programme, grouped under three headings – Talking, doing and recording; Talking and playing games; Carry on talking.
Words and Pictures	No introductory comments. Letter of the week; Things to talk about; Things to make; Things to do; Games to make and play.
Look and Read	The programmes have been planned as a starting-point for work in the classroom, so children will benefit much more from the series if adequate time is given for follow-up work. Teaching content: A choice of language and reading activities.
Stop, Look, Listen	The follow-up work after the series is an essential part of the learning experience. Vocabulary: Themes for discussion; Activities.
Seeing and Doing	Ideas for follow-up – Language: Science and Maths; Creativity.
Watch	After the programme – A full list of various activities.
My World	Follow-up activities – Maths; Language; Art and Craft; Science; Group Activities.

TEACHERS USING TELEVISION

Figure 3.1: <u>Introductory remarks and terms used in the teachers' booklets relating to follow-up and associated activities</u> (Continued)

Series	Teachers' Booklet Comments
1..2..3..Go!	All the suggested follow-up work/activities use either commercial material readily available in the classroom or simple apparatus made by the teacher. Follow-up suggestions (a list of various activities).
Maths-in-a-box	In mathematics, of course, the children learn best by doing and it is as a stimulus to work by the children themselves that the programmes will be most valuable. Suggestions are given for investigation and there are problems for children to solve after each programme. Suggested activities (a list of various activities).
Let's Read... with Basil Brush	The suggestions for follow-up activities, based on the Pepper Stories themselves, aim to help in extending the children's appreciation and involvement beyond the short minutes of viewing. Follow-up suggestions - Talking and Doing (Class); Acting (Groups); Song (Class); Doing (Groups).
Alive and Kicking	The follow-up work avoids subject categorisations but refers to language enrichment, creativity, investigation, discovery and research. Follow-up (a list of various activities).

mentioned. The extent to which this situation prevailed can be gauged from the remarks and terms used in the booklets (Figure 3.1).

Most of these teachers' booklet comments implied that follow-up in a formulated way was essential after programmes had been viewed. They conveyed the impression that television programmes were starting points for children's learning which would be reinforced when follow-up was carried out. As such the preparation - broadcast - follow-up technique was imposed to the detriment of incorporating a programme into the curriculum by integrating it into children's normal activities. In other words, it could be said that the suggestions which accompanied programmes fostered an attitude whereby educational television regulated what teachers did rather than acting as a supplement. This was apparent in the extent that the activities were intended to link with the next programme in the series to provide continuity. However there might have been instances when continuity was not desirable. If the intention were merely to use a story in a broadcast, use a theme of a programme to develop a topic and concentrate on a specific mathematical notion then continuity with the following week's programme would have been immaterial. In such instances, the next week's broadcast might not have been taken as it was either irrelevant to on-going activities or instituted a completely new area of activity. Nevertheless, as learning is a continuous process whereby new knowledge builds-on from existing knowledge and that most language development, mathematical development and topic work necessitate some continuity, it could be expected that in most cases the regular weekly viewing of programmes should provide some form of continuity.

Linking programmes dropped by ten per cent from the third to the ninth week of broadcasting. This was in spite of the Nativity programme in Watch carrying on from the ninth to the tenth week. Continuity appeared to be pursued to a larger extent by teachers of the higher-age ranges than with the lower age-ranges. This was probably because of the serialisation of Robinson Crusoe in Watch, and Dark Towers in Look and Read - each had a high figure for the third week. Nevertheless, the percentage for Look and Read declined as the term progressed. On the other hand, the other language series, Talkabout and Words and Pictures, showed little indication of any link between programmes. The most rapid decline occurred with My World which dropped from sixty per cent for the third week to twenty per cent for the ninth week. The latter figure was in keeping with You and Me, the other general interest programme for the younger children. Stop, Look, Listen dropped appreciably after the third week but the further general interest series, Seeing and Doing, was the only series to indicate any increase in attempts to link programmes. The mathematics series remained reasonably static but 1..2..3..Go! showed some decline while Maths-in-a-Box increased slightly after the third week.

Approximately half of the teachers claimed that programme content was used with other activities they were doing with the children. This gave some indication of whether programmes were separated from other activities or whether attempts had been made to incorporate them into the curriculum. The link between programmes, the information in the teachers' booklet and previewing the programme if a video recorder is available, should place a teacher in a position to foresee how a programme might be aligned or incorporated with other activities. Again, there could be occasions when such integration may be undesirable. This could happen when story is treated as a separate entity, when the mathematical notion is unrelated to on-going activities and when the general interest programme bears no connection to the topic work in progress. The latter type of programme may be taken merely out of interest with no intention to 'follow-up' in any way, but it is questionable whether an unrelated mathematics programme serves any useful purpose. The contents of such programmes are meaningless to children who have not reached the appropriate level of understanding, apart from the fact that those children who have reached the level still need to abstract and rationalise, feats which may be beyond them, if they are to make connections between a programme and their own mathematical knowledge.

These considerations imply that pre-planning is essential for the incorporation of educational television into the curriculum - pre-planning of the series as a whole prior to broadcasts commencing and pre-planning prior to individual programmes to assess how the content and current activities can be combined, i.e. how the content will fit into current activities or how current activities will fit into the content. A third of the teachers asserted that they did plan in advance to incorporate programme content with other activities which were going on in their classroom or in the school. An equal number also stated that events which arose during a programme were used to fit in with other activities. However, these percentages cannot be regarded as separate because in some instances they included teachers in the other category. Figure 3.2 distinguishes between teachers who stated they relied on pre-planning alone, those who pre-planned and used aspects which arose in the programmes, and teachers who did not plan in advance but used material as it arose from programmes.

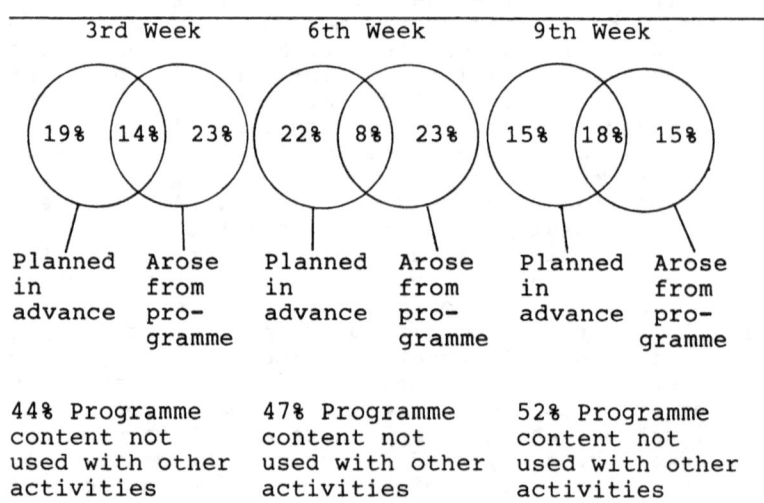

Figure 3.2: How programme content was used with further activities

Twenty three per cent of the teachers relied on material which arose from programmes to use with activities which were going on in the school for the third and sixth weeks, but this decreased to fifteen per cent in the ninth week. This compared with eighteen per cent of the teachers who had already pre-planned but acquired additional material from the programme content. This number was lower for the previous two weeks of sampling.

Teachers of the below five years age-range did not appear to plan as extensively as teachers in the other age-ranges. However they did use content as it arose in programmes more or less to the same degree as other teachers although the percentage declined as the term progressed. Planning by the teachers of the five to six and four to six-years-olds showed a steady decline throughout the term, but teachers of the five to seven-year-olds increased their amount of planning as the term progressed.

The Watch Nativity and Seeing and Doing Hallowe'en programme commanded most planning with other activities, although the sixth week programme in Maths-in-a-Box, The Big Cover Up, which dealt with patterns covering an area, was also planned to be incorporated with other activities. Very little pre-planning appeared to have been associated with the other mathematics series, 1..2..3..Go! As with the below five years age-range, You and Me was not planned to combine with other activities to any large extent and neither were the other general interest series, Stop, Look, Listen and My World. Look and Read was pre-planned for the third week but planning deteriorated afterwards while the other language series, Talkabout and Words and Pictures showed a slight decline over the term.

Although low percentages for pre-planning were indicated for 1..2..3..Go!, programme content was used more for further activities as the term went on. This did not appear to happen with any other series, for they showed a slight decline throughout the term. It is interesting to note however that only one teacher relied on the programme content alone from the Nativity programme for linking with other activities, but twenty nine per cent did so for the Hallowe'en programme. Stop, Look, Listen appeared to be the series which was used least for programme content to arise and be used with other activities.

The explanations which the teachers made of how programmes were used, together with the teachers' booklet suggestions which they found useful to help with further activities, were analysed for the ten weeks of monitoring, and certain anomalies seemed to appear. For example, about fifty per cent of the teachers who monitored language series claimed that programme content was used with other activities they were doing in school. However, the way this was done varied according to the programmes used and in most cases consisted of a direct follow-up. In fact, Table 3.3 indicates that, apart from general interest series, most programmes were used for direct follow-up although it is possible some of the material may have been used later.

There may appear to be a shortfall in the number of checklists received for each series compared to the number expected from ten weeks of

Table 3.3: Distinction of programme use between direct follow-up and other activities

Series	No. of programmes used for direct follow-up	No. of programmes used for linking with other work	Perc. of programmes used for direct follow-up	Perc. of programmes used for linking with other work
Words and Pictures	119	60	66.5	33.5
Talkabout	59	28	67.8	32.2
You and Me	77	17	82.5	17.5
Stop, Look, Listen	13	24	35.1	64.9
Watch	40	112	26.3	73.7
Seeing and Doing	38	48	44.2	55.8
My World	42	22	65.6	34.4
1..2..3..Go!	15	9	62.5	37.5
Maths-in-a-Box	27	5	84.4	15.6
Look and Read	27	5	84.4	15.6

monitoring but it must be borne in mind that Table 3.3 refers only to those teachers who stated they used programme content with on-going activities. In addition, although the group leaders made every effort to secure them, for various reasons a few teachers did not return checklists for some weeks. Other teachers did not take programmes on certain weeks, while some teachers discontinued the viewing of some series. For example, fifty six teachers monitored Words and Pictures and a total of five hundred and sixty checklists should have been expected, but only one hundred and seventy nine were scrutinised. However, only fifty five per cent of the teachers claimed programme content was used for other activities and three teachers had abandoned the series.

Learning Outcomes

It is difficult to assess what children have learned from their participation in an activity. A teacher may feel that certain things have been learned only to find at a later date that this was not so. On other occasions, the teacher will tell children something and expect them to understand and remember but often she finds that her talking has been in vain. Conceptual learning takes place when children have an accumulation of experience that has provided them with the insight to rationalise and interpret these experiences.

The question of whether young children can or cannot learn from television has been discussed previously, but viewing educational television should at least stimulate children to want to learn. Although a teacher has a positive role to play when using educational television, she should also have some idea of the learning which might accrue as a result of programmes being seen by children.

Forty three per cent of the teachers felt that the learning which they anticipated had been achieved, while a further fifty per cent considered that some learning had taken place. The teachers using mathematics series were not as confident that learning had occurred as those using language and general interest series. Nevertheless, there is little variation between the types of series when the teachers who believed some learning had occurred are combined with those who considered that learning outcomes had been achieved - ninety four per cent language, ninety five per cent mathematics and ninety three per cent general interest series. In

Table 3.4: Teachers' estimations of whether or not their anticipated learning outcomes through using educational television series had been achieved

Type of Series	Had been achieved	Some achieved	Not been achieved	No response	Pro forma invalid or not received
Language series	31	43	-	5	22
Mathematics series	2	17	1	-	3
General Interest series	59	46	4	4	18
All series	92	106	5	9	43

other words, a large proportion of the teachers considered that some learning objectives had been achieved through the children watching educational television.

The teachers' explanations reflected the complexity associated with young children's learning. Some teachers evaded the issue with comments such as 'observation and accurate recording', 'many beginnings were made and sometimes they led in unexpected directions', 'the wide age-range of the class implies that different learning outcomes will be achieved', etc., while others merely described what they should have done or what is possible from using educational television. A few teachers however found the question difficult to answer or resented being asked it. These teachers questioned the validity of asking whether learning outcomes had been achieved after only one term's monitoring but the majority of teachers did not appear to be affected. They felt that learning or some learning had been brought about by the use of educational television. Only in instances when series had been abandoned or when, for various reasons, follow-up could not be undertaken, was it felt that no learning had materialised.

The teachers who thought that learning had come about through language series were equally distributed between Words and Pictures and Talkabout with only two teachers using Look and Read thinking so. The teachers were of the opinion that using language series had extended the children's language skills, encouraged them to become more aware of context cues in their reading, promoted a great deal of discussion and brought about an awareness of phonics.

The uncertainty of what is learnt from watching television was emphasised by those teachers who thought that only some learning had occurred. They found difficulty in assessing exactly how much learning had taken place, but general impressions had satisfied them that watching the series had been successful. However, the teachers did not rely solely on the programmes to obtain motivation. They emphasised that the language series were used as reinforcement to achieve learning outcomes, but doubt remained as to whether the objectives had been achieved.

The teachers who thought that learning had occurred through mathematics series only partially substantiated their claims. They considered the series as useful tools to teach children mathematics, and listed various areas of mathematics which they considered the children had learned. These teachers were in contrast to those who thought only some learning had been achieved and who backed up their assertions. The latter teachers remarked that children develop at different rates in mathematics and it was difficult to assess what had actually been acquired. One teacher pointed out that television programmes made mathematics fun but she was not sure as to the extent they assisted mathematical learning. Other teachers stated that some children were at the level at which the programmes were aimed and they believed some learning had resulted.

Reinforcement appeared in two guises in relation to mathematics series. On the one hand, some teachers saw the need to reinforce the aspects of mathematics seen in programmes but other teachers considered that programmes reinforced what the children had already learned. Contrary to the series used for language development, when minimal reference was made to the school's language policy, reference was made by a few teachers to educational television mathematics series fitting in with mathematics schemes, sets of workcards and individual assignments.

There was an absence of explanations by teachers who thought anticipated learning outcomes had been achieved through using general interest series. Most of them implied that programmes had enabled the children to view experiences and instances which usually were not possible and enlarge knowledge of the world around them along with the accompanying vocabulary. According to some teachers, by viewing children extended their language and also showed imagination in creative work. It was further claimed that programmes stimulated children to associate with many of the characters in broadcasts to encourage discussion, vocabulary, finding out and written work while improving their listening skills and concentration span.

Other teachers, although not as affirmative, still lacked a rational basis for claiming that learning had occurred. Programmes were felt to be useful as a visual reinforcement of work being done, a means to stimulate imagination, and encourage language. As a result, the children's work improved because they were interested.

Some teachers who thought that only some

learning had resulted from general interest series appeared to base their views on the effect on the children's language development.

Other teachers gave specific examples of what they considered some children had learned in particular subjects, e.g. mathematics, science, environmental studies, etc. but few referred directly to the learning which emanated from associated topic work. One exception was a teacher using Alive and Kicking who gave good examples of good integration with topic work.

Many responses did not really justify the assertions being made. Confusion appeared to exist between the function of an educational television programme and the teachers' own activity. For instance, a teacher explained that she could never fully anticipate the learning outcomes of any programme because it depended on what part of the programme triggered off the children's interest but she thought a great deal of learning had been achieved by the Nativity programmes in Watch. The assertion that children do not always gain what a teacher expects from a programme or series, but pick on a point which is relatively insignificant, was often repeated. The teachers seemed disappointed that aspects which they had decided were learning areas were missed by the children. Generally, it was felt the programmes had produced interesting written work although follow-up work had proved necessary to emphasise and reinforce points made in programmes.

Involvement with the Project

Although one term is only a short period, the teachers were asked whether involvement with the project had affected their outlook towards educational television. Surprisingly, two thirds of the teachers thought it had, ten per cent were undecided and seven per cent felt no effect. Five per cent of the teachers were previously critical of educational television and had remained so.

It was apparent from the responses that involvement had made the teachers more critical of educational television and how they were using it. The fact that they were obliged to record their actions induced them to evaluate what the educational television series were offering and how they themselves responded.

The teachers had begun to question various features of educational television as it affected their teaching. It was significant that many remarks were made on looking at the teacher's booklet more carefully to determine how better use could be made of programmes, viewing programmes more objectively to ascertain whether the producer was fulfilling his aims, increasing awareness of the different parts, presentation and content of programmes, noticing the reactions of children to programmes, selecting only those programmes which were relevant to the children, not being afraid to miss a programme which was not considered worthwhile, contemplating more adventurous use of the video recorder, considering the purchase of a video recorder, and assessing the role of the teacher when using educational television - before, during and after broadcasts. A few teachers even mentioned that they had thought more about establishing a video library. The usefulness of meeting with other teachers to exchange ideas and suggestions was appreciated by many teachers.

It appeared that the teachers were beginning to make judgements on what they considered beneficial to children's development rather than what was presented by the television producers. In fact, they were starting to question programme content and presentation more carefully and deciding if children would benefit from viewing it. With such a selection of programmes available it was important to carefully select those programmes best suited to the needs of the children and it was easy to fall into the habit of watching a series simply because they always had. This was taken further with comments that reflected that the project had made them aware of the vast resources educational television had to offer and the importance of the teacher's role in taking from programmes what was beneficial and appropriate to the needs of children. In other words, involvement had encouraged the teachers to think about why they used television, what they really got from it and with what kind of children.

Incorporation of educational television into the curriculum was frequently mentioned but mainly in the context of realising how follow-up activities could be better integrated into class activities. However, there were some comments on more thorough preparation before a series began by deciding on a topic and then turning to the teachers' booklets to see if any programmes would offer support. It was further mentioned that greater care would be taken in the choice of series but to this end the teachers would like more previews at a suitable time.

It became apparent to some teachers that it

TEACHERS USING TELEVISION

takes effort, thought and interest on their part to develop the potential of a programme and this involved leading from the children's interests rather than being teacher or teacher's booklet directed. This reinforced another view that educational television can be a marvellous aid but it can also become a 'stand-in' teacher if care is not taken. A teacher may be critical of the presentation and content of programmes but she must consider how she would present the material in question. That teachers must be careful of what children view in school just as parents should be at home and should not let television take over the classroom was a recurring theme.

The analyses of the teacher's role when using educational television led many teachers to look more closely at what the BBC and ITV companies were offering. They felt there were gaps in the types of programmes available for young children, and pointed out how careful compilers of programmes should be in the selection of suitable material. Producers should be aware of the language used for young children and alerted to how important it is that educational television is well produced. There were contentions that some programmes contained too much information for young children to absorb and that educational television should provide material that was difficult for a teacher to acquire. The teachers felt they should be involved and consulted more, both as teachers and parents, in the making of educational television programmes.

The usefulness of a video recorder was reaffirmed by many teachers. They were convinced that a video recording would be more appropriate to use than an off-air broadcast. The children would get more from the programmes. The teacher and the children could talk and discuss during playback rather than at the end of a broadcast. The teacher could assess each programme and decide which parts to omit and which parts would have to be extended in order to give maximum benefit to the children. Programme material could supplement or consolidate other work, and not always in the order in the programme.

These comments provide a different slant to the teachers' attitudes towards educational television than what the findings revealed. However it must be remembered that the conclusions relate to the teachers before they were influenced by the in-service sessions and encouraged to inspect their own practice by completing the checklists.

TEACHERS USING TELEVISION

The changes in attitude illustrate the willingness and eagerness of teachers to improve their practice when given support, but the findings indicate how television is being used in numerous schools throughout England and Wales, and illuminate the extent that eductional television has been neglected in curriculum considerations. As pointed out in Chapter 1, it has received very little attention in official reports and in literature relating to the education of young children. The teachers' comments on their involvement in the project highlight two important areas of concern - (a) the need for HMIs, local education authority inspectors/advisers, teachers' centre wardens and college lecturers to concern themselves more than at present with the role of educational television in the curriculum and (b) the need for an extensive in-service education programme for teachers to take stock and examine whether they are providing adequately for children with their existing practices with educational television.

CHAPTER FOUR

TEACHERS' REACTIONS TOWARDS TELEVISION

Previous discussion has been concerned with the way the teachers were using educational television but it was necessary to ascertain what facilities were at their disposal and whether greater use had been made of them through participation in the project. This was obtained through the final questionnaire which was completed during the summer term, 1984. The sample had reduced from the original two hundred and fifty nine teachers to one hundred and seventy nine. This was attributed to teachers leaving, moving to other schools and local education authorities, dropping out of the project, etc., but also to the sanctions which some teachers' unions operated that term. Attendance at the in-service group meetings was the usual method for returning questionnaires, and some meetings had to be cancelled. This necessitated group leaders making enquiries for the forms to be returned and when this failed the teachers were written to. Many outstanding forms were secured this way but a shortfall of eighty questionnaires remained. Nevertheless, the sample was large enough to base conclusions on.

Teaching Method - Means of Viewing

Possession of Television Receivers

Most of the teachers used a colour receiver for viewing (Table 4.1). Only five per cent of them were restricted to viewing in black and white but there were a number of these television sets in schools. In fact, fifty two teachers (twenty nine per cent) had monochrome television sets in their schools. For almost all of these teachers it was one black and

TEACHERS' REACTIONS TOWARDS TELEVISION

Table 4.1: Number of teachers and the type of receiver they used to view educational television series

Type of receiver	Below 5 yrs.	5-6 years	4-6 years	5-7 years	6-7+ years	All ages
Colour	18	42	24	36	47	167 (93.3%)
Monochrome (Black and White)	1	2	–	3	3	9 (5.0%)
Either colour or monochrome	–	1	2	–	–	3 (1.7%)
Number of teachers	19	45	26	39	50	179

TEACHERS   REACTIONS TOWARDS TELEVISION

white receiver, but one school had four such sets. Apart from the nine teachers still viewing in black and white, only three further teachers sometimes varied between this and viewing in colour. It could be that the other schools retained their monochrome sets in case the colour set broke down. One hundred and twenty eight of the teachers had access to just one colour receiver whilst thirty seven had two colour sets and eight had three colour sets in the school but one teacher was in a school with six colour receivers. These figures indicated the extent that one receiver was relied upon by most teachers and emphasises the problems that this can cause if viewing were at a fixed central point, if the set had to be moved long distances for viewing, timetabling in a large school, etc.

Possession of Video Recorders

The school with six colour receivers did not have a video recorder. Acquisition of a video recorder was not commensurate with the number of sets in a school. In schools with one or two colour receivers, just over a third had video recorders. Half of the schools with three receivers had video recorders. Thirty one per cent of the teachers had access to a video recorder at the beginning of the survey but this had risen to thirty eight per cent within the year, but only a third of the teachers relied exclusively on video playback. The remaining two thirds varied between video recorder use and off-air broadcasts.

Thirty six (fifty three per cent) out of the sixty eight teachers with access to video recorders would have liked to have used the facility more extensively (Figure 4.1) It is noticeable that only two teachers wanted this further use exclusively for timetable convenience. The other teachers mentioned creative use and the opportunity to build up a collection of video tapes within their considerations. The four teachers whose answers did not fall within one of the named categories had other comments to make about the video recorder. They were getting used to using the machine, realising its worth and considering its value for individual interaction. The only problem was that it had to be shared, whereas one television receiver and video recorder to each class would be ideal.

Twenty four of the hundred and eleven teachers without a video recorder did not say whether they felt acquisition of the machine would be of value to

TEACHERS' REACTIONS TOWARDS TELEVISION

Figure 4.1: The facilities which teachers would like to be more extensively provided by possession of a video recorder

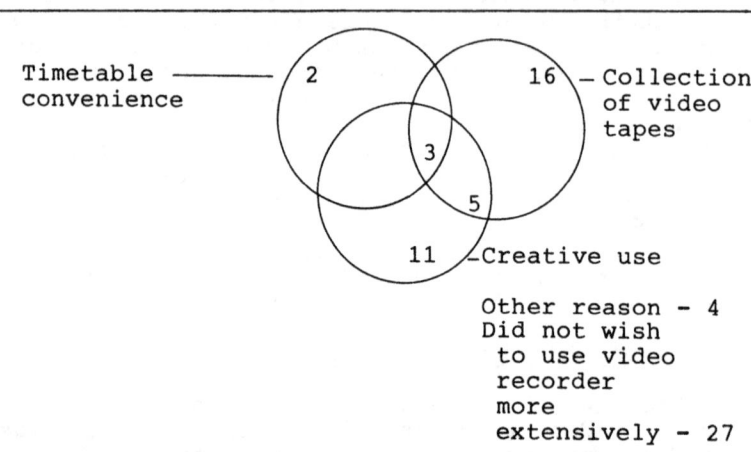

Other reason - 4
Did not wish to use video recorder more extensively - 27

Note: Creative use was classified as use of video techniques such as stop/start and/or integration of programme material into the curriculum

their school. Only six teachers rejected the idea while the remaining eighty one (seventy three per cent) welcomed the idea. A third of these teachers regarded timetable convenience as their priority but nearly a half saw the possibility of creative use. This suggested that many teachers would be amenable to this kind of use if given the necessary support and encouragement. Almost a half of the teachers without a video recorder thought they would obtain the facility in the near future. Whether this was optimism or indicated a trend towards video recorder acquisition cannot be stated. Also, it must be remembered that comments on advantages brought about by using the video recorder occurred constantly during the in-service sessions and some teachers may have been wishfully hoping whereas there was little possibility of their wish being fulfilled.

Changes in Viewing Organisation

Class viewing and mass viewing remained the most common forms of organisation whether watching an off-air broadcast or video playback (Table 4.2). Nevertheless, the percentage of teachers who did so

TEACHERS' REACTIONS TOWARDS TELEVISION

Table 4.2: Means and organisation of children to view educational television

Organisation of children	Used Off-air broadcasts	Used Video recorder	Number of teachers
Whole class/mass viewing	98 (88.3%)	51 (75.0%)	149 (83.2%)
Children from different classes of similar ability viewing	3	2	5 (2.8%)
Small group viewing	3	-	3 (1.7%)
Whole class/mass viewing and children of different classes of similar ability viewing	2	5	7 (3.8%)
Whole class/mass viewing and small group viewing	3	5	8 (4.5%)
Whole class/mass viewing, children from different classes of similar ability viewing and small group viewing	1	4	5 (2.8%)
No response	1	1	2 (1.1%)
Total	111 (62.0%)	68 (38.0%)	179

with video recorders was less than for off-air broadcasts. However, there were a few teachers who alternated general viewing with small group viewing. This appeared to happen with the nursery children and confirmed previous findings.

Nevertheless, whole class and mass viewing seemed to be the exclusive organisation with teachers of the older children and vertically grouped five to seven-year-olds.

Various reasons were given for the advantages and disadvantages of the various forms of organisation, both from the teachers who used off-air broadcasts and those using video playbacks. Some teachers saw advantages in a particular organisation but were aware that it had some disadvantages, but most teachers regarded an organisation as being either advantageous or disadvantageous. There was less divergence among the teachers in respect of general viewing than either of the small group organisations. Some teachers gave several reasons but it was evident from the replies that general viewing enabled the whole class to be together. Eighty four teachers (forty three per cent of those using off-air broadcasts and fifty three per cent of those using video recorders) expressed this view, a further nine teachers considered it was a social advantage, and two teachers said it was the only organisation they had experienced. A further thirty three teachers considered it was beneficial for topic work if the whole class viewed together.

Although it would seem that the teachers were favourably inclined to general viewing, they did have certain reservations about its use. Seventy five of them thought the material viewed was not relevant to the whole class and a further nineteen considered it was difficult to assess what each child had taken from a programme. Seven teachers found organisational problems with general viewing, but a further eight saw no disadvantages and fifty eight did not indicate whether they had any feelings about disadvantages. This probably meant that they had no objections.

These comments suggested that the teachers had mixed feelings about whole classes viewing programmes. On the one hand, it was advantageous to have the children all together, and this seemed to be more pronounced with those teachers who used a video recorder. Surprisingly, very few teachers contended that supervision of the children would have otherwise caused problems. On the other hand, the teachers realised that general viewing was not beneficial for all of the children because programmes were not relevant to some children. The teachers had difficulty in determining what every child had taken from watching. These points were also emphasised at the in-service sessions and many teachers expressed a wish to use small groups but certain obstacles prevented it.

These sentiments were reaffirmed by the questionnaire responses. Fifty eight teachers (twenty seven per cent of those using off-air broadcasts and forty one per cent of those using video recorders) thought the organisation of small groups for viewing too difficult or uneconomic. A further twenty teachers thought the arrangement ideal but not practical and another six were not interested in considering it. Only eleven teachers felt that the organisation offered no disadvantages, while nine teachers were inhibited from adopting it because of lack of staff to supervise the other children or insufficient resources.

Although fifty one teachers gave no indication, only four teachers saw no advantages with small group viewing in their own classes. The remaining teachers indicated that small groups would provide intimacy with the children and enable activities subsequent to a broadcast or video playback to be fitted to individual children. Twelve of the teachers pointed out that small groups would allow children to be organised for viewing according to their abilities but this reason did not appeal to the other teachers.

Nine teachers felt that small group viewing by children from different classes according to ability offered no advantages while a further forty two did not specify their view and fifty seven failed to respond. Sixty six (thirty seven per cent of the entire sample) were in favour of the organisation. They considered that only those children to whom the programme was relevant would watch or that programmes could be used for specific subject areas. Slightly more of the teachers using video recorders were in favour of the organisation. Two main objections were made against it. These concerned the organisational problems the system would cause (fifty five teachers) and the difficulties which would arise with different teachers following-up after a programme (twenty six teachers). These disadvantages were added to by nine teachers who considered the system was not good educational practice with young children and six teachers who were not interested or had not considered it. Only six teachers thought the organisation had no disadvantages. Overall, the disadvantages were seen to be greater by those teachers who used video recorders.

These deliberations on organisation of children for viewing, and how the means at their disposal were used, provided further insights into the teachers' attitudes when using educational television. A slight increase in small group viewing had occurred since the beginning of the project. This might have occurred through awareness brought about by monitoring, and the in-service sessions. However, general viewing still dominated and, it seems, will continue to dominate until teachers are encouraged to release themselves from its shackles. In-service education and support within the school are the only ways to overcome the reluctance by teachers to attempt to change their teaching style and employ small groups. Even possession of a video recorder does not seem to significantly alter the situation. The teachers persist in their former practices with the video recorder being used for general viewing and as a timetable convenience. There were some instances when the video recorder might be said to have lulled the teachers into complacency, i.e. the larger percentage favouring class viewing and considering the organisation of small groups too difficult. Thus, it would appear that in-service courses should emphasise that educational television needs to be recognised as part of the curriculum and its use rationalised to provide greater opportunities for children's learning. The teachers were sympathetic and appreciated the advantages which using the medium with small groups had over general viewing but there was a certain reluctance to amend their practice. Various obstacles were put forward but these are surmountable when a teacher has the will and determination to overcome them.

To change teachers' attitudes when they have become accustomed to something over a number of years is not easy. They need to be convinced that the change is beneficial and is for the good of the children, while their own security with tried and tested ways is being threatened. The responses indicated that teachers treat with caution any change that might interfere with their normal teaching. Moreover, it must be borne in mind that the video recorder is a piece of machinery that is operated by pressing different switches and some teachers are hesitant to use it for fear that they might press the wrong switch or damage the machine.

Educational Television and its Effect on the Curriculum

It would appear at first glance from Table 4.3 that the majority of teachers regarded educational television as supplementing the curriculum or reinforcing work going on in the classroom but the second and third columns provide conflicting evidence. It would seem that there are occasions when educational television either directs what a teacher does or it is treated as a separate entity. Treating it separately seemed to be more common with teachers using off-air broadcasts while teachers of the older age-groups were prone to the medium directing the curriculum. In fact, when asked

TEACHERS' REACTIONS TOWARDS TELEVISION

Table 4.3: How the teachers considered educational television affected the curriculum

	Supplemented and/or reinforced the curriculum	Directed the content of the curriculum	Treated separately from the curriculum
Yes	157	34	32
Sometimes	4	15	16
No	10	116	112
No response	8	14	19
Total	179	179	179

specifically, only five teachers stated that topic work from educational television was integrated with other activities going on in the class while thirty three teachers agreed that educational television directed their topic work and a further fifty one that general interest series generally determined what would be followed-up after a programme. These figures are in keeping with the earlier findings that most general interest series are directly followed up.

This and the previous chapter, have indicated that most teachers do not regard educational television as a curriculum component. It appears to be considered as an alternative yet distinctly separate provision for the children. This seems to be apparent not only from what has been discussed but also from Table 4.4. Two hundred and seventy six comments were made - some teachers gave more than one - and many of them involved some aspects of learning but educational television as a curriculum component seemed to be overlooked. If curriculum is construed as all that happens in a school in relation to objectives, content, organisation, method and evaluation, then it could be said that curriculum is included. For example 'things not available to the teacher' and 'appreciation of things in nature' can be construed as content, but the responses in Table 4.4 appear to lack objectives. The stimulation of curiosity, interest, imagination, discussion and listening skills are anticipated outcomes and objectives to be strived for but these comprise only a quarter of all the responses. It would seem that educational television's greatest benefit according to the teachers is to act as a form of stimulation and to provide material which is unavailable to the

TEACHERS' REACTIONS TOWARDS TELEVISION

Table 4.4: The teachers' views on what were considered the greatest benefits children obtain from watching educational television

Comments	Number of times mentioned
Things not available to teacher can be seen - takes children out of the classroom - widens outlook	79
Arouses curiosity, interest - encourages motivation - presents material in a new way - imagination stimulated	48
Provides visual or auditory stimulus teacher would otherwise find difficult to secure - aids visual or auditory learning	32
Special studio effects aid learning - animation, sound effects, trick photography, graphics, etc.	24
Stimulates discussion and listening skills	24
Another voice or face	19
Helps viewing out of school - shows learning is possible from television	15
Socialisation - group or class togetherness	15
Appreciation of nature	11
Teacher stimulation	3
Children directed to certain parts of programmes	2
Enables parental involvement	2
Builds-up resources	2
Total	276

teacher. There are certain dangers in this. What is being provided need not necessarily relate to children's experiences and, unless the teacher is making provisions, an additional curriculum instigated by television could be introduced. This implies that the children would be following two curricula - a curriculum stipulated by the school and another encouraged by television.

Table 4.3 indicates that a large proportion of the teachers claimed that educational television either supplemented or reinforced the curriculum and directed or was treated separately from the curriculum only to a limited extent. However, previous evidence does not indicate that the medium was incorporated into the curriculum to any great degree. It would seem that change is required in teachers' attitudes to educational television in as much as they should be encouraged to consider its role in the curriculum. If educational television is being used then it is a curriculum component. This implies that its role in the curriculum should be examined to determine what function it should play. Too often educational television is disregarded in curriculum considerations and used at the whim of a teacher. In other words, it returns to curriculum principles and their implementation through the use of educational television, provisions to acquaint students with these during initial training and in in-service courses for teachers, and the need for adequate resources to carry them out. Change to more effective use of educational television will not materialise until attention is given to all of these aspects.

However, the impression must not be conveyed that every teacher of children up to the age of seven years was using educational television ineffectively. The research findings are not encouraging and they suggest that much needs to be done both from production and user points of view but a few teachers were showing what could be done with educational television and how it can be used creatively and incorporated into the curriculum.

CHAPTER FIVE

PRE-SCHOOL CHILDREN, TEACHERS AND TELEVISION

Facilities for Watching Television

Apart from the nursery teachers who participated in the main survey, a questionnaire was circulated in seven LEAs by the local inspector/adviser. One hundred and ten nursery teachers responded. Seventy four of these teachers (sixty seven per cent) had television facilities available, but fifty four (seventy three per cent) were restricted to off-air broadcasts, while the other twenty teachers (twenty seven per cent) had access to a video recorder (Table 5.1). Almost three quarters of these teachers would have had to rely on off-air broadcasts if they had wished to use television. This implies that the children would have watched programmes continuously from beginning to end without interruption. The video recorder was available on a

Table 5.1: The means of viewing television for those nursery teachers who had the facility available

	Off-air	Video Recorder	Combination of off-air and Video recorder
Number of teachers	54 (73.0%)	2 (2.7%)	18 (24.3%)

regular basis to only two teachers while the remainder combined off-air broadcasts with video recorder use. The video recorder was either not available for constant use or the teachers refrained

PRE-SCHOOL CHILDREN, TEACHERS AND TELEVISION

from using it regularly.

Pre School Television Series

Both the BBC and ITV companies broadcast series for pre-school children but the series originate from different departments within the organisations. Broadcasting for children is a BBC tradition. Lord Reith, the first Director General of the BBC, decreed at the very beginning that children should be considered an important audience within a public service system of broadcasting (Home 1983). Radio's Children's Hour became one of the most outstanding broadcasting achievements before, during and immediately after the Second World War. When television became a reality in the 1950s, children's television was automatically built into schedules. It was a visual medium with puppets as well as people. Muffin the Mule was created, and eventually specialised series such as Play School followed. Play School is still broadcast, but BBC Children's Television transmits See-Saw on a regular daily basis at a quarter to two for pre-school children. This slot includes series such as Postman Pat, Bagpuss, Bod, Trumpton, Heads and Tails, Fingerbobs, etc. Pre-school children are provided for by the independent companies on ITV through Rainbow, Pipkins, Let's Pretend, etc. The IBA (1983) state that programmes made specially for the youngest audience aim to help parents and others working with young children to use television as a resource in early childhood education. They add that, despite differences in style and presentation, all of the programmes set out to encourage young children to make viewing part of a wider, active learning experience.

Unless they have a video recorder to record, store and playback programmes, nursery teachers have problems if they wish to use the ITV series, as programmes are usually transmitted at twelve o'clock. This normally means that they are being broadcast during lunchtime and it is inconvenient for the children to watch then. On the other hand, the BBC series are broadcast during school time and are available for viewing. However, problems are created if the nursery is part-time for only the morning or afternoon children are able to view. Furthermore, teachers are also restricted in their planning if they are using Children's Television series. They have to depend on the Radio Times and TV Times for advance information on programmes and neither journal describes the content in any great detail. It is difficult to conceive how such programmes can be incorporated into the nursery curriculum. Programmes might be taken out of interest or to acquaint children with television viewing, but the lack of detail relating to programmes suggests that integrating them within the curriculum is unlikely.

The aim of BBC School Television is to concentrate on those areas of school activity where the medium has most to offer and where it can make a significant contribution which teachers are unlikely to find as well provided from other sources (BBC 1983). The BBC further state that programmes are designed for a carefully defined audience: they are conceived as a resource for the practising teacher and as a stimulus for her pupils; they are, 'generally programmes which include direct teaching or self-study techniques'. This is elaborated by the IBA (op cit) who state that current programme themes reflect teacher demand for resources in both the traditional and new, developing curriculum areas. However, output is planned as much as two years in advance so changes happen slowly, but liaison with schools and educational organisations at many levels help to ensure that programmes match current needs. Consultation between the IBA Education Advisory Council and the School Broadcasting Council of the BBC helps to avoid wasteful duplication of effort and produces a comprehensive and valued educational broadcasting service to Britain's schools and colleges (IBA op cit).

Series Used

Three of the series which were indicated by the broadcasters as relevant to pre-school children were broadcast during 1983/84 - You and Me (BBC), My World (Yorkshire) and 1..2..3..Go! (Central) (See Chapter 2).

The teachers were asked to indicate which series they used, including both educational and Children's Television series (Table 5.2). Three teachers stated they watched five series but this does not necessarily imply that such was on a regular basis. The teachers may have selected between series. Sixty seven per cent of the series used were educational television and thirty three per cent Children's Television. You and Me appeared to be the most popular series, being used by eighty five per cent of those teachers using television,

Table 5.2: The number of television series used by the nursery teachers

	Number of teachers using series (60)	Percentage of teachers using television who used each series	Percentage of whole sample
Educational Television			
Talkabout	8	13.3	7.3
You and Me	51	85.0	46.4
Let's Read with Basil Brush	4	6.7	3.6
My World	12	20.0	10.9
1..2..3..go!	7	11.7	6.4
Words and Pictures	9	15.0	8.2
Watch	2	3.3	1.8
Total	93		
Children's Television			
Watch with Mother	6	10.0	5.5
IBA Lunchtime (Rainbow, etc.)	7	11.7	6.4
Play School	19	31.7	17.3
Seesaw	13	21.7	11.8
Total	45		
Grand Total	138		

Average number of series per teacher using television – 2.3

but the other series listed for children below the age of five years, My World and 1..2..3..Go!, were used by only twenty per cent and twelve per cent of the teachers respectively. This indicated that slightly less than half of the entire sample were using You and Me, eleven per cent My World and six per cent 1..2..3..Go! However, other educational television series that were intended for older children were used by the nursery teachers. Talkabout (a language series), Let's Read with Basil Brush (an introduction to reading series), Words and Pictures (an early reading series) and Watch (a general interest/miscellany series) were also used by certain teachers. A description of these series and how they were used by teachers who monitored them was given in Chapter 3; resorting to them suggests that the teachers concerned were adopting a formal approach with pre-school children.

Nevertheless, the fact that You and Me was widely used gave the impression that a larger proportion of the teachers pursued an informal approach with the children. Although You and Me had certain flaws that did not conform to nursery education principles as described by James (1981), its general ethos encouraged a less structured approach to subsequent activities than the remaining educational television series. The fact that a number of teachers also made use of Children's Television series further suggests television was treated informally by many teachers. It is interesting to note that Play School was the teachers' most popular Children's Television series (Table 4.2) and was considered likewise with a group of parents investigated by Murphy (1983 p.12). Similarly, apart from being the most popular educational television series with the teachers, You and Me was the favourite series with the parents. Strangely, however, Watch with Mother appeared on the teachers' list but not the parents', and this may have been confused with another series.

Reasons For And Against Using Television

The teachers were asked to provide information on why they used television series. The reasons ranged far and wide and included such statements as 'stimulates children to talk about what they see and do', 'normally a follow-up or introduction to particular interest or topic work', 'an educational but enjoyable interlude on a wet day' 'only suitable and enjoyable programmes', 'something different and more like home for those children staying for a school meal', 'simple stories and attractive small books good for sequencing', 'quiet period after dinner', 'to extend range of opportunities offered', introduction of reading and development of language taught and to watch and concentrate', 'to provide the children with something with which they are familiar and confident', and 'exercise in listening'. 'As a way to stimulate the children' appeared to be the main emphasis. There was also support for television extending the range of opportunities offered and as a means to encourage language development. It seemed that the teachers used television for different purposes. Perhaps, in their way, all of them may be justifiable but the fundamental criterion in a nursery school or class is whether the medium is serving a useful function.

The most controversial aspect appeared to be the use and function of television in the nursery. Although the facility was available to seventy four teachers, fourteen did not make use of it, but twenty four of the fifty teachers not using television thought the series being broadcast were suitable for pre-school children. This implies that eighty four teachers, three quarters of the sample, might have used television had it been available to them, and the further quarter had apparently rejected it.

There were three main reasons for declining to use television - the time available to cover all aspects of the nursery curriculum, using television was not in accord with the principles of nursery education, and the influence home viewing was having on pre-school children. The time factor can be understood, particularly in a part-time nursery, when a teacher has many things she wishes to do, but the other two factors need further consideration. Television cannot be dismissed outright. It is part of children's lives. Whether it plays a useful role in the classroom depends on how a teacher uses it. The teachers who rejected it saw television as a threat to the everyday activities of the nursery, i.e. those involving the children in play, encouraging language development, handling materials, engaging in one-to-one communication with an adult, exploring the environment, developing attitudes for the acquisition of concepts and skills, providing problem solving situations, assisting with emotional, physical, social and intellectual development, etc. Television was regarded as a passive activity that would undermine pursuit of these activities. The way some teachers were using television does suggest a likelihood of this happening but much depends on how the teacher has evaluated the role of television, and whether she has rationalised how it fits into the curriculum.

If used astutely, television should enhance the quality of the curriculum for pre-school children. For example, the opportunities to foster language development by hearing stories, songs, poems, rhymes, jingles and finger plays appeared to be the reasons teachers used the medium. If nursery teachers were provided with appropriate series that catered for these, those who did not use television would be missing out on opportunities to supplement children's language acquisition. It was also felt that programmes about nature and animals and everyday experiences to which children could relate would be useful. There was some dissatisfaction with the current series and this might account for some of the rejection of television. Only You and Me emerged as popular, but there was criticism of this series by some teachers who considered it to be too infants' school orientated. There was a strong wish amongst the teachers for a nursery based general interest series. The degree to which current educational television series were not meeting the teachers' needs was reflected in the extent to which the teachers resorted to Children's Television series. Therefore it would appear that there is some justification for an educational television series that is geared specifically to nursery school activities.

A lack of appreciation of the potential of the video recorder might also account for some teachers not using television. Only two teachers used the video recorder exclusively, and even with the nursery teachers in the main sample video recorder use was minimal. This implies that the children were expected to watch off-air programmes continuously for twelve to fifteen minutes.

Home Viewing

The harm thought to be inflicted on pre-school children by watching television at home was emphasised by some teachers and given as their reason for not using it in the nursery. H.M. Inspectorate (DES 1983 p.7) state it would be inconceivable to have television without violence, and go on to add that the news and current affairs programmes must reflect the violent society in which we live, while the drama programmes stand in a tradition many thousands of years old in which violence is a vital element. According to Gunter (1984), hundreds of studies have been carried out and have employed a variety of research procedures to investigate the impact of television violence on the audience. In summarising this research, he maintains that it is important to consider the effect of television in its entirety. Its influence can be harmful or beneficial. Gunter asks, on the level of social behavioural influences for example, is it possible that the effects of pro-social content counteract or cancel out the effects of anti-social content to some extent? Early indications are that whether the net consequences of television viewing are harmful or beneficial depends crucially on the viewer's knowledge about the medium itself and the care with which he or she uses television.

Warnock (1984), on the other hand, maintains that it is insufficient to say that a link between violence on television and real-life violence must exist. We ought to think how this link comes about. There are people who argue that although children may imitate the words and actions of violent television programmes in their play, this has no effect on real behaviour. Some even say that aggressive play is a useful safety valve, reducing aggression in real life. But, Warnock adds, if violent play and violent language go together, it is hard to avoid the conclusion that they may eventually end in real violence. Researchers will say that such gut-based anxiety is insufficient to establish a causal link between watching television and behaviour, and not every child who watches television will become violent. The effects will vary according to character. Some say that only unusually aggressive children are moved to violence by watching it on the screen.

Warnock maintains that an example is not followed unless it is given by someone whom a child admires or loves - someone whose standards they will mirror, whose behaviour in a crisis they will imitate and whose language under stress they will adopt. The lessons of violence therefore are best learned when a child feels at one with the model because then the model is the teacher. It is for this reason that fictional violence is likely to have a stronger effect on children than violence shown on news and current affairs programmes. Such authentic scenes may frighten the timid, but they are unlikely in themselves to initiate the tough into the use of violence. Children are not deeply enough engaged in news and current affairs programmes to be much affected by them. These programmes do not usually supply the viewer with the necessary hero. Only where a model for behaviour may be found are the effects of violence likely to show, especially with very young children. It is of the utmost importance therefore for adults to teach children that violence is wrong. This they can do only by watching television alongside their children and talking to them about the characters they see. If parents cannot or will not do this then teachers must, perhaps the morning after such programmes. It is good use of school time if children could watch again some of the programmes they had watched the night before with the teacher sitting beside them commenting and passing informal judgement on the participants in the drama.

Warnock's sentiments indicate that consideration should be given to television by all those involved with children in pre-school establishments and by those who advise on the running of them. Pre-school children play a great deal at home but they are not dissuaded to do so in nursery school and pre-school playgroups. In fact, play is one of the fundamental aspects of these establishments. Pre-school children might watch a great deal of television at home but shunning it in nursery school and pre-school playgroups is turning away from the reality of the outside world. If one of the principles of nursery education is to help young children develop awareness of the world around them and promote feelings of their identity and place in the world, then educational provisions relating to developmental needs in respect of television should be implicit within the curriculum. This implies that adult mediation is essential when pre-school children watch television. Much of what the children watch on television is not understood and thereby they are more likely to merely imitate what they see (see Chapter 1). Internalization through reason, rationalisation and deduction is beyond their level of mental development so it is essential for someone else, to do it for them, and who better than their teacher.

This presents a new dimension to the role of television in the nursery. Its role in education has usually been associated with formal learning but the previous deliberations suggest that it has a role in informal learning. For such to be achieved requires expeditious use by the teacher, and the previous chapters have indicated that this is not always the case in infants' schools. However, the use of Children's Television and You and Me, together with the reasons for using television that were mentioned previously, suggest that informal learning from television was pursued by some teachers. In fact, a few teachers used this informal learning as a means to proceed to formal learning. This is a prudent way to use television, but there appeared to be many other teachers who did not take this initiative.

<u>Viewing Organisation</u>

Although there was less class viewing by nursery teachers than for any other age range in the main survey, replies on the nursery questionnaire indicated a remarkable increase in small group viewing in comparison, but how this was operated by the teachers cannot be confirmed as they were not visited in their classrooms. Nevertheless, it did appear that discretion was used by a number of teachers when using television but the situation became somewhat blurred when responses to who normally watched with the children were given. It appeared that both the teacher and nursery assistant watched television with the children in the majority of instances and this implies that the other children were left on their own if small group viewing was operated. Circumstances are somewhat different in a nursery than in an infants' school classroom. Infants' children can be assigned various activities while the teacher is occupied with the group watching television, but nursery children are apt to move more freely from one activity to another. Perhaps the situation is different in the nursery when the teacher does not emphasise preparation, has no teachers' booklet to abide by and uses a programme for enjoyment and interest. As quoted earlier, broadcasts in most instances were continuous but the teacher and nursery assistant could have been watching a programme with a small group of children while keeping an eye on the other children. If something was amiss, either of the two adults would have left the television to attend to it.

PRE-SCHOOL CHILDREN, TEACHERS AND TELEVISION

Learning Outcomes

Although the children's enjoyment of watching television was a primary consideration by the nursery teachers, to some extent formal learning was associated with using the medium. This was particularly noticeable with the lack of reference to play emanating from watching television and the extent to which programmes were followed-up. It is possible that, as play is such an accepted part of the nursery curriculum, the teachers assumed it would be taken for granted that it was implicit in further activities or followed-on when opportunities arose at an appropriate time. On the other hand, the intention to pursue specific learning outcomes, especially by the main survey sample, suggested otherwise.

As instanced earlier, the nursery teachers considered language development as the most important aspect of the curriculum to arise from watching educational television. Although the teachers were not in favour of specific language series, they wanted programmes of a general nature from which language could be developed. Programmes were considered a means to assist with the extension of vocabulary, an aid to sentence structure and intonation. Stories, songs and rhymes that could be depicted by animations, cartoons, puppets, etc. were considered a valuable source of motivation and some teachers regarded this as the main function of educational television for pre-school children.

However, no evidence was found of programmes being incorporated into the curriculum, but nursery teachers do normally regard language as being implicit in mostly everything carried out so there was no need for any exception with television. It was just another activity in which language would incidentally occur. Likewise, the story element in a programme could be regarded as just another activity and did not require specific attention for it to be incorporated in the curriculum.

Nevertheless, it is implicit in any learning situation that activities should be at the level of development of the learner, and the nursery is no exception. Language development is individual to each child and the teacher must make provisions accordingly. Furthermore, there was evidence that a few teachers were resorting to general interest series intended for older children. Although topic work was not necessarily followed, the series appeared to be beyond the level of comprehension for

PRE-SCHOOL CHILDREN, TEACHERS AND TELEVISION

nursery children. Moreover, the teachers' booklets for the series provided ideas and suggestions for formal follow-up activities. Although these series were used to acquaint children with aspects of their world in addition to being used for language, this situation re-emphasises the need for a suitable nursery based series. You and Me and My World do not appear to be fulfilling the function. My World was accused of being too formally based and did not conform to activities associated with the nursery. The teachers' booklet was subject based and oriented towards activities more appropriate to older infants' school children. Despite its popularity, You and Me was not wholly satisfactory. Some observations relating to the series were mentioned previously but additional comments were made by the nursery teachers. The songs and stories were thought to be good, the participation of Duncan the Dragon and Purrfecta the cat provided opportunities for the children to be involved and the emotional effect of some programmes was appreciated, but other aspects were considered of little value. Certain events in programmes were beyond the understanding of pre-school children, too much conversation by the puppets Cosmo and Dibs slowed down programmes and 'tried to stretch moral values a bit too much',upper case letters and names instead of the sounds of letters were often used and there were no indications of where the stories and songs in programmes could be found.

Mathematics was not excluded from the considerations for a general series for nursery children. Although the infants' school teachers indicated a preference for specific mathematics series, the nursery teachers preferred a combination of mathematics and general interest series. However, despite this preference, it seemed that development in number took priority in mathematics, and shape, size, estimation and measurement were relegated to lesser significance. The attitude was reflected by the choice of the mathematics series, 1..2..3..Go!, as a means to reinforce number work. Furthermore, there appeared to be no attempt to incorporate educational television mathematics programmes into the curriculum. Eleven teachers indicated they followed a mathematics scheme in their school and educational television programmes were not regarded as part of the scheme.

Whole class viewing appeared to be the popular form for organising the children to view programmes relating to mathematics followed by discussion before the children were assigned to tasks. Language was believed by many teachers to be an integral part of mathematics and emphasis seemed to be placed on its acquisition. They considered that the children would benefit from hearing the correct vocabulary during programmes.

The teachers appeared to rely on direct teaching and language acquisition from educational television to encourage mathematical development. This was in spite of contentions that pre-school children acquired mathematics through experience and that play and the environment were fundamental to the experience. However, 1..2..3..Go! was a studio based series and gave little indication of exploring mathematics in the environment and neither My World nor You and Me provided this experience. The teachers complained of a lack of series which could be used for mathematics, and the emphasis on specific aspects of mathematics in a general series would be more in keeping with the principles of nursery education.

Television in the Nursery

The situation with pre-school children, teachers and television seems to be in need of attention. The first aspect to be tackled should be the teachers' role. Television has not been regarded as within the province of the nursery so teachers and advisers have not been concerned. However, the preceding evidence suggests otherwise and indicates a need for serious consideration to be given to its function in the nursery. This will be achieved only when those responsible for deciding on nursery education policy take the matter into account. This should include every aspect of television as it relates to nursery children - informal learning, formal learning and home viewing. Once this has been resolved, teachers must be challenged to consider the role and function of television in the curriculum, i.e. how television is used to its best advantage to supplement both informal and formal learning, how the effects of home viewing are dealt with, the implementation of small group or casual viewing, the sharing of responsibilities between themselves and the nursery assistant when television is used and which programme material is most suitable to use. Consideration of these matters will involve introducing the issues into initial training and the setting-up of in-service courses for serving teachers. Practitioners cannot be expected to rationalise television within the nursery curriculum unless they are given guidance and support in examining the issues involved.

Teachers will require sufficient resources if they are to use television effectively. This will mean the provision of adequate equipment and appropriate programme material. They should have a television receiver and video recorder at their disposal. This recommendation may cause consternation in certain quarters. Nursery schools and nursery classes do not receive an over-generous capitation allowance and cannot be expected to raise sufficient money to buy the equipment. But if television is thought to be of sufficient concern to warrant consideration in the nursery curriculum (the aforementioned comments on its present use, future use and potential use, and matters related to home viewing suggest that it is) then funds should be made available. In fact, consideration should be given to whether one video recorder and receiver is sufficient if a teacher intends to record BBC and ITV broadcasts. These development and change issues are discussed in Chapter 7, but provision of suitable programme material is fundamental to the medium being recognised as integral to the curriculum.

Previous remarks have indicated the need for an educational television series specifically geared to the nursery and based on nursery education principles. You and Me comes nearest to this but it is not completely fulfilling the need. Although similar in content in many ways the series for the nursery should have a different bias. It should not be closed with specific goals but open to enable nursery teachers to use their professional expertise. As such it would not require a booklet containing ideas and suggestions but a full synopsis of programme content to enable teachers to decide how the material might be used. Obviously, the booklet will not be so necessary if a teacher has a video recorder because she would be in a position to preview the content to select what she would use and how she would use it.

The criterion to be borne in mind when considering television material for nursery children is that an adult mediator is essential when using the material. This would entail content being presented in such a way that the adult would need to act as intermediary between the television receiver and the children. Broadcasts at the moment are construed as programmes with continuous transmission. There is no reason why broadcasts should not be modular to allow adult intervention at appropriate intervals to enable one aspect to be dealt with for a few minutes only. Moreover, the modular approach is adaptable and conducive to use with a video recorder (see Chapter 7).

Above all the series should not attempt to teach skills. The objectives should be to lay the foundations for the future acquisition of skills together with the formation of concepts, development of auditory and visual discrimination, development of concentration and reasoning powers, and the provision of emotional and social experience. If these objectives are to be secured then the content must be open for teachers to use according to the needs and experience of the children, and to be incorporated within the curriculum. Stories, songs, poems, rhymes and finger plays should feature in the series. Some broadcasts could be given over entirely to these aspects but stories should be told by a skilled storyteller and should include well known and well liked stories as well as any suitable new material. The material should consist of incidents with which pre-school children can associate and these should consist of fewer studio based sequences and more events and situations from the environment. Television can provide close-ups of visual material of natural things which cannot be obtained in other ways. Puppets, cartoons, animations, camera tricks, etc. should be used with discrimination and included only if they are fundamental to the event being portrayed.

To provide such series needs the co-operation of many people. The BBC School Broadcasting Council and IBA Educational Advisory Council, assisted by a Pre-School Panel, have overall control of policy but it is worth considering whether a new Council should be formed to supervise and control educational series for pre-school children. This body could advise, supervise and control the making of pre-school series, and consist of educationalists, nursery teachers, parents, childminders, playgroup personnel, and others with experience of pre-school children. The arrangement would ensure that the content side of educational television series for pre-school children is the prerogative of those concerned with the education of the children, while the production and technical side would be the responsibility of the producers who, after all, are experts in their field.

REFERENCES

BBC (1983), BBC for Schools, London. BBC.
DES (1983), Popular Television and Schoolchildren, London. Department of Education and Science.
Gunter, B. (1984), Television and the Young Viewer - Separating the Potential for Good from the Potential for Harm, The Head Teachers Review, Spring, pp. 8-10.
Home, A. (1983), Children's Television and Its Responsibilities: The Producer's Point of View, in "Learning From Television: Psychological and Educational Research", ed. Howe, M.J., London. Academic Press, pp. 193-201.
IBA (1983), Learning Through Television, London. IBA
James, C. (1981), A Curriculum Framework for the Nursery, Early Childhood, 1, pp. 14-17.
Murphy, C. (1983), Talking About Television: Opportunities for Language Development in Young Children, London . IBA.
Warnock, M. (1984), The Television Trap, Women and Home, November, pp. 70-71.

CHAPTER SIX

TELEVISION AND CURRICULUM CONTENT

Educational television should be used as a resource to fit in with what teachers are attempting to achieve with their children and this is bound to vary from school to school. As Murray (1983) stated, curricular relevance is centrally important to the use of broadcasts. Thus, educational television cannot be divorced from curricular considerations but regarded as a resource or a supplement to teaching. It is then possible to identify objectives within subject areas and elucidate principles with which educational television should conform.
The pilot work had indicated that language, mathematics and topic work were the range of programmes of interest for teachers of children up to seven years of age. Therefore questionnaires were designed to ascertain how the teachers in the main survey related educational television to these. As explained in Chapter 2, the questionnaire used, the related tables, summary in depth of the responses and implications resulting from these are reported in Choat, Griffin and Hobart (1987). This chapter contains those matters which have a direct bearing on the use of educational television as it relates to these areas of curriculum content.

Language

As nearly ninety-one per cent of the teachers used educational television to help with their language teaching (Table 2.2), coupled with the tone of the responses discussed in the previous chapters, it appears that teachers of children up to seven years of age regard language as one of the most, if not the most, important areas of the curriculum. The teachers are complying with the objectives of

TELEVISION AND CURRICULUM CONTENT

English teaching as expressed by the DES (1984 pp.2-3) which states that the aspects of language competence which should occur in pupils' experience of using language are in speaking, listening, reading and writing. This statement implies that attention should focus on language development and the acquisition of language skills. Language development is interpreted as the increase in capability to structure language to achieve explicit meaning through agreed sounds which symbolise objects, processes, relationships, etc. to facilitate a common interchange between persons through interpretation of the symbolised form. On the other hand, language skills are the structures which have to be learned to be able to produce and receive the symbolised forms.

The responses from the two hundred and twenty seven teachers who completed the language questionnaire suggested that teachers of the younger children regarded educational television as a means to increase children's vocabulary by encountering words which they would not normally use, to extend sentence structure and to help with intonation. Teachers of the older children considered educational television as a stimulus for discussion, a means to help broaden children's vocabulary, encourage creative writing, develop listening skills and concentration through hearing clear, spoken language. Therefore both sets of teachers had views that emphasised children's use of language. Their expressed emphasis was directed towards language development rather than the acquisition of language skills. Yet analysis of their use of educational television programmes indicated that the emphasis was in practice reversed by most teachers, with attention directed towards language skills. The questionnaire replies indicated that direct teaching from educational television was the common teaching method. They were, as some teachers apologetically mentioned, resorting to 'chalk and talk'. Only with the nursery class teachers was diversion detected, but even then a structured follow-up was evident with oral work on a class basis to recapitulate events in a programme, to explain words, sing songs and recite poems.

Encouraging discussion was considered very important by fifty six per cent of the teachers and important by a further thirty three per cent. Helping with decoding skills, reading with understanding and encouraging writing held some importance throughout the age ranges, apart from the below five years of age group where it was not emphasised. Further evidence which stressed the skill emphasis arose from those teachers who indicated a preference for language series. This was especially prevalent with the teachers of the older children. Language series were appreciated for assisting with the teaching of basic skills. The series were considered useful for presenting language rules in a way that made them interesting, introducing sounds, sound blendings and phonic word building, looking at discriminations between letter sounds and letter shapes, focusing on reading strategies such as sight vocabulary, phonic skills, language patterns, etc., and covering word building, use of tenses, punctuation, etc. Thus, language series were regarded as a means to deal with language conventions and reading skills.

On the other hand, general interest series were felt to provide opportunities for extending language and were considered more stimulating for the purpose than language series. Consequently, it appeared that general interest series were more conducive to language development but language series were regarded as suitable for learning language skills. A fifth of the teachers preferred both types of series, a third preferred general interest series only, while forty five per cent preferred language series only, but these proportions were somewhat misleading. Forty three per cent of the educational television series used for language teaching were language series while forty nine per cent were general interest series and a further eight per cent mathematics series (Table 2.2).

The aspect on which there was almost total agreement concerned stories, songs and poems. The teachers regarded stories, songs and poems as an integral part of educational television for the added interest which these gave to a programme, as a stimulus to encouraging children to read, as an assistance to acquiring listening skills, sequencing, sense of rhythm, concentration and memorisation, as an enrichment to children's imagination, as a distinction between the spoken and written word and, above all, as an enjoyment. In fact, stories, songs and poems were the main reason for some nursery class teachers using educational television. Therefore it seems that stories, songs and poems were regarded as a means to foster language development rather than language skills and this appeared to be the case with Talkabout. The stories in the series, and how they were portrayed,

TELEVISION AND CURRICULUM CONTENT

acted as a stimulus to enrich and extend children's vocabulary, develop the powers of imagination, give experience of a variety of language styles and usage and to promote discussion. The teachers thought the stories and songs enjoyable and interesting and, apart from language development, led to many other activities. Very little of the integration was attributed to the teachers' booklet suggestions, for only just over a half of the teachers made use of it.

This reaction to Talkabout contrasted markedly with Words and Pictures and Look and Read which were selected by teachers primarily to foster language and reading skills. A few teachers only made use of the story in Words and Pictures, but the majority followed-up the suggestions in the teachers' booklets to develop skills through discussion, reading and writing activities, and in many instances through use of the accompanying worksheets. In fact, as quoted in Chapter 3, the Look and Read teachers' booklet encouraged this attitude by suggesting that adequate time after watching programmes should be given to follow-up in the skills. Moreover, nearly a third of the top infants' class teachers used Look and Read which really is a junior school series. Furthermore, Words and Pictures was the most widely used of all the language series, being particularly popular with reception class teachers (sixty five per cent), teachers of four to six-year-olds (eighty one per cent) and teachers of five to seven-year-olds (sixty one per cent). On the other hand, Talkabout was used by only forty four per cent of reception class teachers and forty five per cent of teachers of four to six-year-olds. Meanwhile, Watch was used by sixty one per cent of teachers of five to seven-year-olds and sixty five per cent of top infants' teachers. Of the other general interest series, only You and Me with the nursery children (sixty eight per cent) and Seeing and Doing with the five to seven-year-olds (twenty eight per cent) exceeded twenty five per cent in their use for language development. However, thirty two per cent of the nursery class teachers used Let's Read with Basil Brush, a further twenty six per cent Words and Pictures, while twenty one per cent used Talkabout.

Although these viewing figures suggest that nursery teachers do place emphasis on language development, it must be pointed out that no specific language skills series is broadcast for nursery children. However, once children reach reception class age language skills appear to over-ride language development, as instanced by the popularity of Words and Pictures compared to Talkabout and the general interest series. Of course, some allowance must be made in respect of the content and format of Talkabout and My World (the relevant general interest series) because these series may not have been liked by some teachers. The language and reading skills emphases seem to persist with the older infants' school children when judged by the extent that the teachers resorted to the junior school series Look and Read (thirty per cent) and the degree to which Words and Pictures was still used (thirty nine per cent). This indicates that sixty nine per cent of the teachers of six to seven-year-olds were using series to further the acquisition of skills but it must also be pointed out that general interest series, especially Watch (sixty five per cent), were being used for language (Table 2.2). Nevertheless, although the figures suggest fairly heavy use of both language and general series, less than a fifth of the teachers were prepared to combine them, and even then separation between the development and skill aspects was evident. The teachers considered that the series complemented each other - the language series providing for the structured approach necessary to learn the skills and the general interest series providing opportunities for the linguistic groundwork for development of oracy. Not one teacher suggested a change to incorporate what was sought from both types of series into one series. Furthermore, a half of the teachers were content with the series which were being provided for language and saw no need for change.

Although twelve per cent did not respond, fifty nine per cent of the teachers insisted they were reinforcing the language policy of the school when using educational television, while a further fifteen per cent claimed it was incidental but indications were that reinforcement was the emphasis. To justify their actions, the teachers claimed that they used only the series that backed up work already going on. Only a small proportion, fewer than four per cent, felt the language policy was influenced by educational television. It would seem, therefore, as if educational television is primarily used for the support that it gives to the acquisition of skills, that the language intention of most schools for children up to seven years of age is skill orientated. The possible exception might be nursery classes where language development

TELEVISION AND CURRICULUM CONTENT

appeared to dominate.
The emphasis towards skills is not surprising. Thomas (1985 pp. 15-16), when investigating ILEA primary schools, also reported an over-emphasis being placed on skills. He concluded that schools were undemanding when they concentrated too much on skills and the achievements earned were at too high a price in relation to the rest of the curriculum, while the attitude was also detrimental to the children. By virtue of what it is presenting, the support material available, how the material is interpreted and the use made of it, educational television appears to be influencing teachers in their attitude towards language and reading skills. Teachers may maintain that educational television reinforces their school's language policy, but the evidence in Chapter 3 of the direct follow-up attitude, lack of continuity between programmes and separation from other activities suggests that educational television is often isolated from other aspects of the curriculum and also indicates an absence of planning by most teachers.

It would appear that educational television is acting as a catalyst in relation to language teaching. Apart from the nursery classes, skill teaching predominates and this is being aided and abetted by the educational television material. In other words, by the types of series being broadcast and the support material accompanying them, educational television is encouraging teachers to believe they should perpetuate the learning of language and reading skills at the expense of trying to foster language development. This is despite the teachers' claim of general interest series being used for the purpose and the greater use of this type of series than the language series. Diagnosis of the data, together with the findings reported in Chapter 3, indicated a lack of evidence to suggest that general interest series were being used to any great effect to enhance language development.

This conclusion was reached irrespective of the claims by nearly two thirds of the sample that children were catered for individually when using educational television. As pointed out previously, it is difficult to envisage how this can be achieved when children are class or mass viewing. The teachers maintained that individual needs could be ascertained through discussion when each child contributed his ideas on what he had seen in a programme and when appropriate work was assigned to him according to his ability. It appears that teachers are placing too much faith in the value of discussion. They are assuming that young children are able to perceive in a programme what they perceive and ignoring the fact that they are the interpreters between children and educational television. Children may focus on completely different action in a programme from that which a teacher wants to discuss while she has to convey meaning of what the action depicts. This implies that interpretation should be immediate if it is to be significant to the children, whereas most discussion takes place after a programme has finished. In other words, as most broadcasts are treated continuously from beginning to end without a pause, teachers are disregarding the time lapse of a fifteen-minute programme. Thus, although a child may participate in discussion of an educational television programme, it does not imply he has acquired the necessary relevance to understand the activity assigned to him.

Only eight per cent of the teachers in the sample agreed with these views. In contrast, just over a quarter felt that individual needs and experiences in language could be catered for through educational television, while a half thought there were some limitations. The former teachers thought that the visual stimulus encouraged children to look, listen, and think, and that television was a substitute for the lack of experience in many children. It was believed the children were taking things from programmes and were acquiring vocabulary not previously encountered. The latter teachers were not quite as assured. Although they believed that individual language needs and experiences could be met through educational television, much depended on individual programmes and how individual children reacted to them.

The inevitable question in relation to language indicated by the preceding evidence is whether educational television material should be geared towards language development or acquisition of language and reading skills. If the principles advocated by Thomas (op cit) and others are to be adopted to encourage language development then revision of the existing provisions has to be undertaken. This may involve changes to existing series or even replacing them with new series. Alternatively, there may be a case for retaining certain series, such as Words and Pictures and Look and Read, but liberalising the teachers' booklets so that these do not encourage uniform follow-up with completion of worksheets, etc., while broadcasting further series which emphasise language development. This is a case of which teachers want is not necessarily what teachers need. It may appear by their popularity that Words and Pictures and Look and Read are what teachers want but the way the series are used suggests this is not what they need. They should be provided with material which will encourage imaginative use and flexibility rather than being made to feel obliged to have to comply with the teachers' booklet recommendations.

The compromise would be series which emphasise language development and provide some opportunities to include language and reading skills for those teachers who wish to pursue them. This would mean four series, one each for reception, middle and top infants, and a further series for nursery children. Further consideration should be given to a series for children for whom English is a second language. Two series, Words and Pictures and Story Time are now (1985/86) broadcast for infants' school children, and You and Me for nursery/reception children. The recommendation would either replace these series or amend these series and add a further two series. It is also worth considering whether changes could be made in the current general interest/miscellany series to accommodate two new language series. At present, four such series are broadcast - Watch, Seeing and Doing, Stop, Look, Listen and My World - while a further series, Thinkabout, has a science base but claims to provide for language development. Although the teachers claimed that these series were used for language development, the prior evidence did not suggest this was achieved to any great extent, but some teachers made the suggestion that advantage should be taken by producers to develop general interest series more fully to allow scope for language and mathematical development. In fact, it was felt that the general interest series were a 'bit old fashioned' and in need of revitalisation.

Whatever form any new language series may take, there are certain essentials which should be considered. Stories, songs and poems should play an important role. These were considered the basis around which language development could emanate if aided by the technical possibilities available to producers. Programmes should not be repeated as frequently as they are at present. Producers should concentrate on a particular theme without trying to put too much into programmes, the programmes should be at a pace appropriate to the developmental level for which they are intended, and relate to experiences common to the children. Concern should be given to the choice of presenters and whether it is wise to include children in programmes. The emphasis should be to create a feeling for the love of language and this can be achieved only when presenters display the same feeling. Apart from attitude, care should be taken to ensure that the language used in programmes is an acceptable language, and language depictions on screen should follow the same principles. Care needs to be taken that lower case letters only are used in series intended for children at lower developmental levels. Programmes should not rely on a single format but be varied while being constructed in such a way that they link from programme to programme. They should include open-ended questions, especially bearing in mind the possibility of stop/start use with the video recorder. Above all, with the teacher as interpreter, programmes should provide opportunities for children to analyse, make judgements and add comments to become participants and not passive viewers.

Mathematics

Several features related to language reoccurred with mathematics but further issues also arose. Compared to the ninety one per cent who used educational television for language, only thirty seven per cent of the teachers used the medium for mathematics. Dissension was attributed to lack of time, lack of suitable series, difficulty of presenting a mathematics programme to children of different abilities and rejection because of educational principles. Whereas educational television was considered suitable for language development, there was a certain amount of resentment against it for mathematical development.

The provision of suitable series is a controversial issue. Some teachers may regard series as suitable if their content is orientated towards the direct teaching of mathematics and are accompanied by material which provides many follow-up suggestions. On the other hand, other teachers may regard series as suitable when they inspire children to become involved at their level of development through practical activities which lead to mathematical understanding. The latter teachers would align with those teachers who rejected

TELEVISION AND CURRICULUM CONTENT

mathematics series on educational grounds and who believed that mathematical concepts are created and not taught. This implies that this group of teachers regarded patterns of relationships as the basis of mathematical development. They believed mathematics was individual to children and that concepts resulted from direct experience and practical activities. Although a further group of teachers regarded mathematics as individual, their obstacle was providing for individuality through a broadcast. This implies that these teachers were not able, or were not prepared, to fit programmes to individual children and suggested that they too declined to use educational television for mathematics on educational grounds. The teachers who gave their reason as lack of time also reflected their attitude to educational television and mathematics. Time would have been found if they had thought it worthwhile. In other words, educational television had insufficient attraction to be used for mathematics and time which would have been spent on watching a broadcast was used for other things.

Despite these reservations towards mathematics through educational television just over a third of the teachers (almost equally divided between those who did and those who did not use educational television for mathematics) gave an explicit reason when asked what they thought a good educational television programme could do to help with mathematical development. These teachers believed educational television could show that mathematics was exciting, practical, implicit in the environment, and a common language. The medium could provide opportunities for the extension and application of ideas within children's understanding to encourage practical activities for the eventual acquisition of concepts. Thus, educational television was not regarded as a means for direct teaching but to support and extend activities already begun by the teacher. However, the teachers thought that educational television was limited in what it could do owing to the abstract nature of mathematics, and mathematical stimulus could be better provided in a good general interest programme. This indicated a disinclination for mathematics series but it was not entirely borne out by the teachers who used the medium for mathematics. Slightly more mathematics series than general interest series were used (Table 2.2), but the percentage might have been greater if the unit on Reflections in You and Me had been included.

Moreover, account had to be taken of the language series which were also used for mathematics, and this appeared to consist mainly of Words and Pictures (Table 2.2).

Further analysis also revealed that teachers of the younger children relied on 1..2..3..Go! and You and Me, but ignored My World, which mentioned mathematics in the teachers' booklet, while teachers of the older children were almost equally divided in the use of Maths-in-a-Box and Watch, with the other general interest series ignored. Furthermore, a curious phenomenon seemed to surround Maths-in-a-Box. Twenty seven teachers used it for mathematics but twenty eight for language and twenty three for general interest. It could be argued that this was thirty eight, fourteen and fifteen per cent respectively but every teacher had the opportunity to use the series for all three disciplines and this amounted to twelve per cent for each.

Together with the fact that twelve teachers used 1..2..3..Go! for language and eight for general interest, the figures suggest that these teachers believed educational television mathematics series would provide young children with the appropriate mathematical language. In other words, emphasis was on language rather than practical activities for children to acquire mathematics.

It would seem that mathematics and educational television have an uneasy co-existence. Rejection occurs for a number of reasons, but when educational television is accepted it is not being used to good effect. It is being used as an alternative method to teach mathematics rather than encouraging young children to create mathematics for themselves through experience. Moreover, it does not appear as if the medium is being used to foster mathematical development to any great extent. The main emphasis seemed to be instrumental learning of mathematics. This attitude was reflected in what the teachers considered the most valuable parts of programmes. Very few of the favoured points referred to patterns of relationship. Most were concerned with number by specific teaching e.g. counting animals, matching words to counting, grouping tens by sandcastles, Punch and Judy counting backwards, story of one-to-one correspondence, etc.

Furthermore, although the total of language and general interest series used for mathematical development exceeded mathematics series (Table 2.2), just over a half of the teachers expressed preference for specific mathematics series. They contended that mathematics series were structured and geared towards a specific mathematical notion whereas general interest series only offered incidental mathematics learning. These views stress a formal attitude towards mathematics possessed by the teachers when using educational television. Fewer than a fifth of the teachers felt mathematics could be adequately catered for by general interest series and a further fifth by a combination of mathematics and general interest series. But, as with language development, none of the teachers suggested a change in format to incorporate both types of series. They considered each as being necessary.

The situation is more confusing when environmental factors are considered. Encouraging looking for mathematics in the environment was considered very important by the teachers of the older children and bringing mathematics in the surroundings into the classroom was regarded as the most important thing educational television could do. However, no indication of this happening was given by the teachers who monitored a mathematics series when the number of occasions other activities were pursued after programmes was investigated. In fact, the only occasions when the environment appeared to feature in the teachers' activities were a few instances which related to Stop, Look, Listen but these did not refer specifically to mathematics. This suggests that although general interest series may provide environmental sequences it does not ensure they will be taken up for the children to actually explore mathematics in the surroundings. This is further substantiated by the nursery teachers who thought encouragement of shape and size development of little or no importance and who, together with the reception teachers, considered estimation and measurement development of little or no importance. However encouraging number development held some importance at least for all the age-ranges.

Furthermore, two thirds of the teachers felt that educational television should encourage mathematics through play but the response was inconsistent throughout the age-ranges. The nursery and four to six-year-old teachers were firmly convinced, but the remaining age groups indicated some indifference. However, the monitoring results gave little evidence of play occurring when teachers used programmes. Some play arose from You and Me and to a lesser extent with My World, but 1..2..3..Go!

TELEVISION AND CURRICULUM CONTENT

and Maths-in-a-Box did not encourage any play whatsoever.

Children should be regarded as individuals if progress is to be made in mathematics and this arises when opportunities are provided to enable them to acquire experiences. The teachers were not convinced that this could come about through using educational television. The medium was regarded as a means of stimulation by showing situations familiar to children to demonstrate mathematics in action but there were limitations. Television may lead to activities in which children might not normally participate and sometimes a topic might lead to activities with a mathematical connection, but emphasis remained on the teacher. Educational television was of value only when the teacher guided children through a 'good follow-up'.

Nevertheless the majority of the teachers appeared to be allowing educational television to influence their mathematics teaching by accepting what the broadcasters were providing and following-up with the teachers' booklet suggestions. This acceptance resolved into a pre-determination of what they expected children to learn by fitting them to the content of a programme and this was reinforced afterwards by following-up with directly related activities. In other words, there was little concern for developmental factors when using educational television for mathematics. However, nearly a quarter of the teachers claimed they combined educational television with their mathematics schemes. This was possible owing to the flexibility of the scheme to enable programme content to be fitted in or because the content filled gaps in the scheme. Almost all of the remaining teachers did not align broadcasts with their mathematics scheme. Programmes were independent of the scheme, there was no set plan or the teachers were indifferent about it. This suggested a lack of planning by the teachers to incorporate educational television into the curriculum but interpretation of 'mathematics scheme' also has to be taken into account when contemplating this conclusion. Only a third of the teachers had a specific scheme drawn up by the LEA, school or themselves. A further fifty five per cent used a particular mathematics text book or set of workcards but these cannot be considered as a scheme. They do not abide by a philosophy for children's acquisition of mathematics or consider the psychology of learning mathematics according to children's levels of development. They merely

TELEVISION AND CURRICULUM CONTENT

concentrate on mathematical content, often in a linear order.

The foregoing comments indicate some disturbing features relating to educational television and mathematical development that must be considered before attempting to elucidate principles. Several teachers were not in favour of what is currently being presented, further teachers rejected the medium because of educational principles and many others who were using it appeared to be doing so for wrong reasons. Only a minority seemed to be using educational television broadcasts effectively.

Emphasis was on learning mathematical language and stipulating learning tasks with play and environmental experiences ignored. These criticisms indicate a need for teachers of young children to question their approach to mathematics teaching. Perhaps television can assist by transmitting in-service series for teachers, but until this happens, producers must be cautious in what they are presenting in series for children. Womack (1984) was critical about this and was concerned that producers' views of content and presentation of mathematics series might not align with those of teachers.

The teachers were asked whether they thought changes were necessary in the present provisions for mathematics. Almost a half did not reply but this included most of the teachers who were opposed to using educational television for mathematics. The teachers who felt no changes necessary amounted to nearly eleven per cent whereas thirty two per cent thought some changes desirable and eight per cent wanted many changes. These figures suggested some disapproval of the present provisions for mathematics.

Although disapproval appeared to exist, it amounted to a mixture of dissatisfaction with programme content and dissatisfaction with policy. The teachers felt that programmes in the present series were not clearly defined and that they were an assortment of unconnected parts lacking specific goals. They maintained quite strongly that only one mathematical notion should be dealt with for a period of a few weeks rather than jumping about from one thing to another in programmes. This would avoid too much detail being included and allow programmes to be transmitted at a pace appropriate to the children. Children's normal surroundings should be used as the basis of programmes to provide a natural flow and to reduce the number of studio sequences.

TELEVISION AND CURRICULUM CONTENT

This would also enable mathematics to be created and would lead to investigative work. Series should last for three terms rather than two terms as at present and be transmitted weekly and not fortnightly. These recommendations emphasise the necessity to consider the role of mathematics in general interest series. With the facilities available, broadcasters should use locations and situations not accessible to teachers to enable teaching to be supplemented. It was also emphasised that programmes should be presented by a person who knew something about mathematics for young children to enable a feeling towards it to be encouraged.

While acknowledging that mathematics was fun and exciting, it was also felt that programmes should not resort to gimmicks and lose the mathematical emphasis. The teachers also thought that an imbalance existed between the provisions made for language and those for mathematics. Those in favour of mathematics on television believed that greater emphasis was placed on language, with many series geared towards it, while mathematics was largely neglected. Some of this neglect could be attributed to the failure by the broadcasters to evolve a suitable formula to transmit material conducive to young children's mathematical development. On the other hand, the nature of mathematics could be the cause. Being a discipline which has to be created and is based on abstractions and generalisations, it was difficult to conceive how these abstractions and generalisations can be portrayed for young children to abstract and generalise themselves. As a result, the attempts which have been made rely on direct teaching in the belief that the viewer will make the necessary deductions and rationalisations to acquire realisation of the mathematics involved. This may be possible with individuals who have reached higher levels of thought development, but is impracticable with young children who are predominantly at the pre-operational level.

The only way to overcome the dilemma is to present situations on educational television that will encourage the acquisition of mathematics. These should be open ended, although recognisable by the teacher, to provide practical activities for children. In this way, mathematics is a doing not a watching activity and educational television is acting as a supplement to motivate both teachers and children. Obviously, the medium is used to much greater effect to achieve this if a video recorder is used with only a small group of children who have been selected according to their needs. In fact, educational television has a potential for assisting young children's mathematical development that has hitherto been unexplored. With the possibilities offered by enterprising use of the video recorder, and research to establish how material can be presented to comply with the principles outlined, educational television has an exciting future to play in helping with young children's mathematics. But this will not come about unless there is complete co-operation between broadcasters, educationalists and teachers.

Topic Work

While the teachers indicated that they regarded the provision of material for language development or class discussion the most important reasons for viewing general interest series, they also attached importance to other areas of the curriculum. Although there was some suggestion in the in-service sessions that there may be some justification for specialist programmes in areas such as science and music, the general consensus was that reading, language and mathematics should be taught separately and the rest of the curriculum content integrated and taught by a centre of interest or topic approach. A topic, of course, would also include work in language and mathematics when it arose. The difficulty of catering for the different needs of children and ensuring that all areas of the curriculum are being covered has been referred to previously. Nevertheless, the large majority of teachers prefer this type of approach and it is the system used in nearly all infants' schools. The teachers who comprised the sample were representative of the general opinion and practice.

However, how this practice is implemented varies widely between schools and teachers within schools. At one extreme there are teachers who have no particular plan for topic work but use children's interest to decide what should be taught. In contrast to this there are schools where all topic work is carefully planned and schemes of work are provided for teachers to follow. Between these extremes there are schools which allow teachers to choose whatever topic they like (which means that topics are sometimes being repeated) and schools where topics are decided by consultation between teachers and the headteacher. Most of the teaching

TELEVISION AND CURRICULUM CONTENT

is modified in practice. Teachers in schools that seem to have fairly rigid programmes of work would claim that they would cater for a child's particular interest even if this were not part of the planned topic, and they would modify or even drop a topic if effective teaching was not resulting. Also, teachers who rely on topics emerging from children's interests claim that preparation is necessary for this and that sometimes interests are encouraged. Other teachers, while admitting that topics may be repeated, would claim that teachers approach the work in different ways and different teaching results.

What does seem evident is that such an important area of work should be carefully planned. The booklet by Essex County Council (1983) suggests that a written document should be produced in each school to ensure that important points are considered during this planning. It was not possible during the survey to determine to what extent this planning did take place but it did seem that educational television was considered only when a unit was specially designed for the purpose or when this happened to coincide with a topic being taught. Although a large proportion of teachers, especially those teaching the older children, used these units, only a few are considered suitable for use in this way and none of these is considered suitable for children under six years of age. It is interesting that the document referred to previously, while excellent on most accounts, only devoted two lines to the use of educational television, although it did ask the important question if, when television is used, does it tend to dictate what is taught rather than ensure integration into the curriculum?

The responses to the topic work questionnaire suggested that a large number of general interest series were used as a basis for topic work, especially amongst older children. However, this was accounted for by one particular series and fortuitous use when a particular programme happened to fit in with work the teachers were doing. This occurred quite frequently during Hallowe'en and before Christmas. There were some instances of a particular programme providing the stimulus for topic work but these were infrequent and had not been prepared beforehand. Although general interest series did tend to produce more variable work than language and mathematics series, the direct follow-up approach was used in the majority of cases. This often had no connection with what was being taught otherwise. Topic work based on a particular unit did produce some varied and enterprising work but, in some cases, the suggestions in the teachers' notes were followed closely and this resulted in a series of follow-up lessons. The teachers did find the notes very valuable for topic work.

While it must be accepted that time is limited in infants' schools where teachers have a full-time teaching commitment, it does seem necessary that, if full advantage is to be taken of educational television's possible use in topic work, time must be spent to see if programmes in any of the series would be useful as part of a planned topic. This does not apply just to general interest series as there may be suitable programmes in the language or mathematics series. Suitable titles could be obtained from the annual programme guide and further details from the teachers' or children's booklets. This was rarely attempted by the teachers and the impression was gained from the in-service sessions, and the topic work questionnaire that this was because of the way teachers traditionally used television rather than the time involved. The IBA have recently issued a pamphlet with programmes categorised under topic headings; it will be interesting to see how much this is used.

Thirty one per cent of the teachers had access to a video recorder but this made only a little difference in the use of educational television in relation to topic work. Some programmes were recorded and used on later occasions, and there were only a few cases of previewing to decide whether programmes were suitable. There is great potential for the use of the video recorder for topic work. Programmes could be shown at the most appropriate times and could be seen as a whole or in part on later occasions. They could be stopped or started to explain relevant points and certain sections seen by part of the class who were involved in that particular aspect of the topic. This occurred infrequently amongst the teachers who were surveyed.

For the above considerations to be fully effective, schools need a large video tape collection or should be able to obtain relevant tapes from local Resource Centres in the same way as they obtain other resource material, i.e. pictures, books, etc. This presents many problems and it must be said that of the schools which participated in the survey only two seemed to have sufficient resources and only one LEA seemed to be able to supply sufficient material for schools from the local Resource Centre. There were a small number of schools which were starting to build up their collection of videotapes.

Careful planning must take place to make effective use of educational television for topic work. Sufficient resources i.e. receivers, video recorders and tapes, should be available and obtained if deficient. This will not come about, however, until all concerned with education adopt a positive attitude towards educational television which, at present, only a small number of educationalists and teachers hold.

REFERENCES

Choat, E., Griffin, H. and Hobart, D. (1987), Language, Mathematics, Topic Work and Television, Beckenham, Croom Helm.

Department of Education and Science (1984), English from 5 to 16, Curriculum Matters No. 1, London. HMSO.

Essex County Council (1983), Topics and Centres of Interest in the Primary School, Chelmsford. Essex C.C.

Murray, J.F. ed. (1983), Broadcasting and the Curriculum, Glasgow: Jordanhill College of Education.

Thomas, N. (1985), Improving Primary Schools, London. ILEA.

Womack, D. (1984), Maths on Television: Viewing or Doing? London. IBA.

CHAPTER SEVEN

IMPLICATIONS, CHANGE AND FUTURE DEVELOPMENT

Video recorders are numerous in nearly all secondary schools and are increasing in number in primary schools, while interactive television is a development that must warrant consideration in the future. However the previous chapters indicate that not many teachers were using television effectively. A few teachers were incorporating it into the curriculum, following-on with the children rather than following-up, taking small groups of children to watch programmes or parts of programmes and, when video recording facilities were available, using the machine to preview, to stop/start, freeze frame, play-back, play forward, etc. Not all of these teachers were adopting all the practices. Some were using only one or sometimes two of the facilities.

It is not surprising that educational television has been neglected in nursery and primary school curriculum considerations. Television was established domestically long before it was introduced into schools, and habits gained during home viewing were transferred into the classroom. Broadcasts were received off-air just as they were at home and everyone sat around the television receiver to view them. Teachers had to justify why they gathered children around a television set because others might have thought that they should have been more gainfully occupied. Consequently, it was considered prudent to provide evidence to show that time had not been wasted, and a system was instituted whereby children were prepared for what they were about to watch and follow-up with appropriate work once a broadcast had finished. Accompanying booklets were prepared by the broadcasters to provide ideas and suggestions to help teachers. The previous chapters have indicated

IMPLICATIONS, CHANGE AND FUTURE DEVELOPMENT

that the procedure has not changed and remains the common practice with the majority of teachers of children up to seven years of age, even though some of them have the use of a video recorder. The video recorder was used mostly for time-table convenience; a programme could be recorded and shown at a time which suited the teacher. Neither did there seem to be much effort from teachers to preview programmes before they were shown to children. Playback of a programme was treated as if it were an off-air broadcast and viewed continuously from beginning to end. The stop/start mechanism was rarely brought into operation. Very few schools had considered the possibility of setting-up a resource bank of video tapes and programmes were retained only in exceptional circumstances. The common practice was to record those programmes required in the current week and re-record the following week's broadcasts on the same tape.

Consequently, possession of a video recorder has had little influence on how educational television is used by most nursery and infants' school teachers. Although teachers insist that, within nursery and primary education, children should be regarded as individuals to cater for their emotional, social, physical and intellectual development, this does not appear to be happening when it comes to using educational television. Only a few examples of small group viewing were instanced and these were mostly with mathematics or watching a general interest series in nursery classes. The majority of children were taken as a class, joined with another class and sometimes with other classes, to watch educational television.

There might be some excuse for class viewing when a teacher is restricted to off-air broadcasts, when the children have to be taken to someone else's classroom or the hall to watch a programme, when there is only one television set in a school, etc., but there is little justification for mass viewing. Most programmes are broadcast twice a week and only in an exceptionally large infant's school should there be more than two classes needing to watch the same series. This implies that each class would have the opportunity to watch the broadcast on one of the occasions and should be timetabled accordingly. The teachers claimed that this was often not possible owing to the use of the viewing area for other purposes, other timetable commitments, another teacher wishing to watch another programme at the same time, etc.

IMPLICATIONS, CHANGE AND FUTURE DEVELOPMENT

The direct follow-up of programmes, lack of continuity between programmes and separation from other activities suggested that educational television was isolated from other aspects of the curriculum. Little evidence was found that teachers planned in any great depth. The preparation-broadcast-follow-up technique was imposed to the detriment of incorporation into the curriculum through integration in children's normal activities. The teachers' booklet suggestions seemed to implant the attitude that educational television regulated what the teachers did rather than acted as a servant to them. Together with the closed format of the programmes, it appeared that educational television was influencing and, in many instances, directing a great deal of language, mathematics and general interest teaching. The extent to which this was applicable can be gauged by the fact that ninety one per cent of teachers of children up to seven years of age were using educational television to assist with language development, thirty seven per cent with mathematical development and eighty four per cent for general interest. The degree of use is not disputed for Miss Sheila Innes, BBC controller of educational broadcasting, is reported by O'Connor (1985) as stating that the reason so many children built igloos in the snow was attributed to a Watch programme because eighty per cent of primary schools took the series. Miss Innes is further quoted as saying:-

> "We do not control the curriculum but we like to think we influence it. And perhaps the best thing we can do for institutional education at the moment is offer some enrichment in areas which may be becoming impoverished at local authority level."

According to Bates (1984a pp. 18-19), enrichment is perhaps the most common term used to describe the use of school broadcasting but it is rarely defined. But, Bates adds, British broadcasting organisations are able to get a pretty good idea of the needs of schools and the shift of opinions and trends through their advisory councils and education officers. Later (p.47), Bates indicates that it is difficult to see school broadcasters moving away from programmes of the enrichment type because these reflect the same styles and approaches to programme-making found in general television. He further states (pp. 233-235) that broadcasting's

IMPLICATIONS, CHANGE AND FUTURE DEVELOPMENT

real potential for meeting special needs in schools has been largely unexploited because the broadcasters are not expert in these areas and have not used their advisers to the full. Educational broadcasters, many of whom started out as teachers, are to some extent caught between different professional ideologies and a spectrum of approaches that will be found in any educational broadcasting department. The existence of independent, professional broadcasting organisations, with their own career structures and methods of rewards separate from the educational system, is a major obstacle to a freely integrated team approach.

Bates' remarks, and the deliberations on how educational television was being used, indicate that some changes are desirable but these cannot be contemplated unless principles and policies that should underlie educational television for young children are ascertained.

Some ineffective use of educational television can be attributed to the failure to consider it as a curriculum component. Curriculum these days refers to all the learning which is planned and guided by a school, and embraces objectives, content, method, organisation and evaluation. Educational television affects all of these considerations but it has been regarded merely as something extraneous to the curriculum and left for teachers to use at will. According to Ryder (1985), most teachers do not consider educational television as central to the curriculum and regard it as peripheral to their teaching. They contend that education is acquired through human interaction and television is devoid of this. This interpretation implies that television can teach, children can learn from merely watching it, and teachers have no responsibility to moderate between the television set and children. In fact, the project's findings confirm that this attitude, although not consciously applied, was widespread among teachers but the allegation that educational television is peripheral is not entirely true. Teachers may state it is peripheral but the previous figures indicate that it is used extensively for language and topic work and, to a lesser degree, for mathematics. The figures, supported by Innes' claim, suggest that educational television is far from an incidental curriculum element. Educational television is more than an aid to teachers in the education of young children than hitherto suggested. It should be a resource and supplement within a teacher's provisions for learning.

IMPLICATIONS, CHANGE AND FUTURE DEVELOPMENT

If television is not recognised and accepted as a curriculum component, the implication must be drawn that a teacher is following two curricula - one stipulated by the school and the other encouraged by educational television. Inspectors, teachers' centre wardens, college lecturers, head teachers and teachers should re-think their attitudes towards educational television to bring about changes that will result in more effective use of the medium to incorporate it into the curriculum. The changes appertain to teachers in their professional role and to areas of the curriculum:-

Initial Training

Very few colleges at the moment include a course on educational television in their training of teachers. The medium is treated as something teachers will adopt and adapt to in the course of their teaching. Without guidance and awareness of the implications surrounding the use of educational television, it is only natural that students resort to what they feel is the way to use it when they become teachers - merely taking children to watch programmes. They would benefit from a course that emphasised how their teaching could be supplemented by the use of television, the role of the medium in the curriculum and its relationship to children's learning.

In-Service Education

The fact that very few colleges provide training in the use of educational television must have a bearing on teachers' ineffective use of the medium but the situation has not been corrected for the majority of teachers since they qualified. Very few in-service courses have been held at teachers' centres and colleges or have been sponsored by the DES. The use of educational television has been ignored on the assumption that television is a simple thing for teachers to use. They have been left to get on with it by themselves and only those who have evaluated the implications of their use of the medium have contemplated change. Even so, these teachers have been left to their own devices, often without the support and encouragement of people in higher positions. The existing situation reveals an urgent need for an increased in-service programme to acquaint teachers with ways in which educational television might be used more effectively with

IMPLICATIONS, CHANGE AND FUTURE DEVELOPMENT

existing resources and to embark on more enterprising teaching by accepting some of the developments taking place.

Resources

A further cause of the ineffective use of educational television can be attributed to the resources available to teachers. Often with only one television set at their disposal, a possibility that the aerial point may be in the hall or someone else's classroom, the television set having to be moved around the school, fixed times for viewing, etc., contribute to the lethargy with which television viewing is associated. It is essential, if good standards of teaching are expected, that teachers should be provided with the appropriate equipment to achieve these standards. This implies that schools should be equipped with sufficient television receivers, video recorders and other material to meet their needs. Financial provisions should be made available to assist schools to purchase new material and equipment when developments occur. This has been feasible with the micro-computer and should be made available to other forms of technology.

Objectives

Changes in the use of educational television should be considered in the light of whether they will enhance children's learning. Little is known of what young children do learn from watching television but interpretation through the teacher and active participation by the children are necessary if opportunities for learning are to be enhanced. Teachers must plan and decide how educational television is to supplement the provisions she is making for children's learning and for it to be recognised as a curriculum component. They will need to take into account what could be gained from using educational television in areas of the curriculum, when it will be judicious not to use it and how usage fits in with curriculum policies of the school.

Content

It is inevitable that the content of an educational television series, and programmes in the series, must warrant a great deal of consideration

IMPLICATIONS, CHANGE AND FUTURE DEVELOPMENT

within teachers' objectives. Without the appropriate content in programmes, objectives cannot be achieved. Although many teachers did not wish for changes in the current series, much of this apparent satisfaction can be misleading. The majority of teachers were not using the material to the best advantage. The video recorder was being used to perpetuate the view and follow-up syndrome and this was encouraged by the format of programmes and suggestions on follow-up in the teachers' booklets. Not one primary education series has been adapted to cater for use with a video recorder. Each programme is continuous and, according to Jelley (1984), "television producers wish to continue to make programmes and enjoy the prestige of making nationally broadcast and viewed programmes". This premise results in closed programmes which constrain teachers to follow the aims instituted by the producer. Instead, there is a need for open material that will allow teachers to use it as they require and to select only parts of the material that align with children's needs. Teachers' booklets should be changed by including details of the content to allow teachers to plan prior to broadcasts to incorporate the material into the curriculum. This implies a reduction in the number of follow-up suggestions and indicates that teachers should use their own initiative to cater for follow-on according to the children's needs, interests and current activities. In other words, change should ensure that educational television, in any of its guises or forms, is not regularising what teachers should do and thereby influencing their attitudes to teaching. Teachers should remain the controlling influence and be selective in the material they use. They should cease to use educational television if their control is being eroded.

These content changes suggest that the policy and production aspects of educational television series need greater involvement from persons outside broadcasting. The BBC Schools Broadcasting Council and IBA Educational Advisory Council are restricted in that they only oversee and approve plans in general and do not vet the content, format and presentation of series during the planning and production stages. Series, and programmes within them, should be devised in conjunction with practitioners and others with educational expertise, which only happens to a limited extent at present. This implies that the policy and educational side of production would be vested in educationalists, and

IMPLICATIONS, CHANGE AND FUTURE DEVELOPMENT

the technical and television side would be the broadcasters' responsibilities. Educational television is an educational service and under these arrangements would be within the jurisdiction of those whom it serves. In this way, programme content would be more aligned to curriculum requirements and the controlling consortium more attuned to implement curriculum change.

The need to change the existing controlling format is exemplified by the way programmes and teachers' booklets are influencing, and often directing, what is being taught to young children. Language development was being sacrificed to language and reading skills. Teachers were encouraged to have children completing worksheets instead of allowing them language experience opportunities. Some language series were trying to cover a too wide developmental spread, relying too heavily on the same format and were repeated too frequently. There was a very strong emphasis that more stories, songs and rhymes of quality should feature in programmes, that language development should be given more consideration in general interest series, that language should be developed by presenting programmes about children's everyday life and environment, and that the whole of the language provisions needed restructuring. Changes too were required with general interest series. These should contain units lasting four to five weeks that could be suitable for topic work, the children should be able to relate what is shown to their own experiences, programmes should not attempt to be too technical, serious, complicated and confusing while being at a pace suitable to the children. Moreover, general interest series should not over-emphasise follow-up with too much formal work but be inclined to foster practical activities and play. Number seemed to be the over-riding emphasis of mathematics series. Dissatisfaction was expressed as to the objectives of the series being broadcast and it was felt that too much effort was made to directly teach children through programme content. Some of the content poorly depicted mathematics and there was little effort to encourage children to define patterns of relationship. The series did not awaken mathematical enquiry or the pursuit of mathematics in subsequent activities. They were considered to be too fragmentary and without clearly defined goals. Change was thought desirable to a format which would concentrate on just one mathematical topic for three or four weeks

IMPLICATIONS, CHANGE AND FUTURE DEVELOPMENT

and without too much being crammed into each programme. This should enable a natural flow to be achieved that concentrated on activities in children's normal surroundings, would enable creative activities to be associated with programmes and provide opportunities for investigative work. This would also allow teachers to plan activities at different levels for children. Furthermore, as with language, more could be done in general interest series to include mathematics.

Organisation

The prior comments have indicated the need to encourage change in the viewing organisation practised by a large number of teachers. There can be no justification for young children to be subjected to mass viewing if one of the principles of nursery and primary education is to treat each child as an individual. Teachers may claim that they follow-up individually but this seems difficult to achieve with either class viewing or mass viewing. They cannot ascertain what each child has taken from viewing or interpret to each child individually. There are certain circumstances that may restrict change but every effort should be made for only those children for whom it is relevant to view a programme or part of a programme. This implies small group viewing for language and mathematics programmes and for some aspects of topic work. Obviously, resources play a major role in the feasibility of this viewing arrangement. Ideally, each teacher should have her own television set and video recorder but such is never likely to materialise. As a compromise, schools should be equipped with two television receivers and two video recorders - one video to be used for recording during broadcast time and available for playback afterwards, and the other video recorder available for playback at all times. A few teachers were practising small group viewing with off-air broadcasts and they must be admired for their efforts, but the video recorder is the obvious answer.

Method

Once teachers are provided with adequate equipment and suitable programme content, there is no reason whatsoever for not changing their teaching methods when using educational television. Although

IMPLICATIONS, CHANGE AND FUTURE DEVELOPMENT

it is rather more difficult to implement change if use is restricted to off-air broadcasts, it is still not out of the question. The first priority is to dispense with the preparation-broadcast-follow-up technique and structured follow-up to incorporate educational television into the curriculum. This will necessitate taking note of programme content and using only those programmes which are relevant to groups of children. The other children, to whom the programme is irrelevant, can continue with other activities. This arrangement implies that a teacher must be selective in choosing the appropriate material and for this she depends on detailed programme synopses in teachers' booklets. Alternatively, if the whole class views an off-air broadcast, the teacher must plan how a programme will be fitted to each child's needs. Over-emphasis on class discussion should be avoided. Children should follow-on with practical situations in their normal activities or with individual interaction with the video recorder.

Change in method is much simpler when a video recorder is acquired. The teacher can then adopt small group viewing as and when she requires it, but the video recorder introduces a different style of teaching. By previewing what has been recorded, a teacher can select sequences in programmes and use only those with particular children. Material can be stored on tapes and used when it is required to fit in with children's activities. During a playback, the teacher can stop the video recorder to observe, describe, question, elaborate and discuss. She can go back to show a sequence or event again. The children too can ask to have certain aspects repeated. Hence, the teacher is acting as interpreter and a three-way interaction between teacher, children and television is established. No longer are lengthy episodes necessary and no longer are the children passive viewers. They are active and participating, and through their involvement are being encouraged to think and learn. The teacher has greater opportunity to select those children to whom the extract is relevant in the first place, and in the second place to deal with the children on an individual basis. She can observe each child's reactions, the aspects which have interested them, note where interpretations are necessary and ensure appropriate follow-on activities according to each child's needs. Moreover, the teacher can be involved with this small group whilst the other children in the class are engaged in other activities.

IMPLICATIONS, CHANGE AND FUTURE DEVELOPMENT

The video recorder also enables interaction to be extended when only one or two children use the machine. Operating a video recorder is within the capacity of some young and most of the older infants' school children as many now have video recorders in their homes. The teacher can assign them to obtain certain information from the video tape and suggest various activities when this information has been procured. Again, the children are involved and required to think, observe and analyse. Obviously, the task must be appropriate to a child's developmental level and it should not require rationalisation or deduction in any great depth. Thus, it would appear that finding the correct word, copying captions, asking simple questions of a 'what happened when' nature would be the limit of what children up to seven years of age could undertake with the present facilities.

Evaluation

Through attendance at in-service sessions, teachers will be encouraged to inspect their practices with educational television. Moreover, in many instances they will not only be evaluating their practice with educational television but their teaching as a whole. They will be encouraged, and hopefully stimulated, to consider how they are using educational television, whether it is making a worthwhile contribution to the curriculum, if programme content can be used more advantageously, whether organisation and teaching methods can be changed to provide greater learning opportunities for the children, and consider whether adoption of developments will enhance their teaching.

These considerations emphasise a need for clear and unbiased thought when evaluating educational television and the curriculum. According to Choat (1980, pp. 108-110), evaluation does not make statements about recipients but about the education service being provided. Evaluation measures teaching input/output and cannot be implemented unless recognisable objectives exist on which achievement or non-achievement can be based. The selection of objectives, demands judgement of what it is hoped can be achieved. The curriculum should be such that evaluation indicates whether the means are providing attainment of the objectives. A school should have certain achievements, attitudes, values and interests that it is encouraging its pupils to acquire, and these can be obtained only by providing

IMPLICATIONS, CHANGE AND FUTURE DEVELOPMENT

appropriate experiences for the children. Therefore it is necessary to constantly evaluate objectives, content, organisation and method, and the nature, extent and direction of changes which might have taken place. Consequently, realistic objectives are essential if account is to be taken of children as individuals in a school or class. Objectives are successfully evaluated only when each child is considered as an individual, and children vary in their ability, growth, personality, interests, needs, home background, etc. Evaluation of educational television in the curriculum should indicate how use of the medium is catering for these.

However desirable changes in the use of, and principles associated with, educational television might be, they cannot be considered separately from developments which have occurred in recent years. The video recorder has been the most significant development. Furthermore, a number of teachers regard acquisition of a video recorder as the means to overcome their problems with educational television. Indeed, educational television becomes a different proposition when a teacher has free access to a video recorder and when she uses it wisely. As stated previously, she can preview programmes to select which sequences are applicable for certain children to view, have prior knowledge of any aspect which may need clarification, be aware of which elements require interpretation and be prepared for vocabulary that may present difficulties to the children. In other words, the teacher is controlling what a playback is going to provide rather than being obedient to what an off-air broadcast dictates. Television is supplementing her teaching but she is using it in the way and through a means that she feels will enhance children's learning with a different approach than practised with an off-air transmission.

When the material for use has been selected, and the children gathered for viewing, the teacher has autonomy when showing it. The sequence can be stopped and started at appropriate junctures for interaction by herself or the children. A particular frame can be frozen to act as a still picture to encourage further interaction, the rewind mechanism allows a return to a particular sequence for clarification or repetition, and the fast-forward control permits aspects not required to be by-passed.

The stop/start mechanism appears to be the most

IMPLICATIONS, CHANGE AND FUTURE DEVELOPMENT

useful function of the video recorder. Instead of playing through continuously, the teacher is able to intervene and bring the children into the proceedings rather than having them watch passively. The playback may be in progress for only a minute or even less before the teacher wishes the children to interact and she can repeat the process as many times as she wishes. Furthermore, the children are able to ask for the tape to be stopped or played back for something they wish to see again. Used in this way the video recorder has distinct advantages over conventional broadcasting for as Bates (1984b) states, broadcasts are ephemeral in comparison to video tapes, cannot be interrupted or stopped, are transmitted at fixed times, are single-paced, self-contained and dense in information. On the other hand, cassettes can be used when convenient and appropriate, reviewed segment by segment, and structured in a wider variety of ways than broadcasts. They give teachers and children greater control and can be used for mastery learning, reflection, analysis, interrogation of evidence and individual learning.

Nevertheless, Bates (1985) intimates that children often dislike a programme being interrupted and ideally it should be played through first without interruption, then stopped at three or four points for questions and discussions. When a teacher takes control of the medium by directing the video playback, the children soon become accustomed to this alternative way of viewing. As Bates acknowledges, video material made in a modular format is still relatively rare, but television has an advantage over books or computers in that a great deal of information of different kinds, i.e. pictorial, emotional, factual and subjective, can be packed into a half hour tape and a lot of ground covered in unpacking this information.

Schools have the opportunity to set up resource banks of video tapes for use when a particular aspect is required by teachers. As Bates (loc cit) further indicates, this material can be used in exactly the same way as reference material in a library when selected extracts relevant to teaching needs are used. This can be done by using appropriate material from several tapes or editing the extracts on to one cassette. Apart from easing the recording and playback arrangements mentioned earlier, the latter method also necessitates having two video recorders in a school. Recording programmes off-air and editing mean more work for

IMPLICATIONS, CHANGE AND FUTURE DEVELOPMENT

the teacher responsible, while there is the task of cataloguing the material. According to Betts (1983, pp. 69-70), each blank video tape, recording made and completed programme edited from a recording should be given an individual number with its own record card stored in a central file. Each recording record card should show the tape number, the date the recording was made and any comment about the technical quality of the recording and playback. Each programme record card should indicate the recording number, the number of the tape on which the programme is currently recorded and an indication of the title and content. Betts adds that it may seem cumbersome having three record cards that need to be cross-referenced but it aids quick retrieval of information and is worth the trouble of starting and keeping them up to date.

Establishing and maintaining a recording and cataloguing system is an arduous task when teaching in a small infants' school or nursery school. These teachers get very little free time, if any at all, are busy teaching for most of the school day and usually preparing both before and after school. This implies that any recording and cataloguing must be fitted into a tight schedule, and it is not surprising that very few schools have managed to set up a resource bank of video tapes. The common practice is to record programmes on a weekly basis, erasing and recording on the same tapes in following weeks. Programmes are retained only if they are of special importance, i.e. The Nativity, Hallowe'en, Pond Life, etc., or if it is the last transmission of a particular programme. Moreover, not many infants' and nursery teachers are technically minded, and most lack the necessary back-up, while many schools have insufficient funds to procure a large stock of tapes. The shortage of money also precludes schools purchasing a quantity of commercially produced tapes, if they were available, as an alternative to recording off-air broadcasts. This implies that schools for young children will be obliged to rely on recording off-air broadcasts for some years to come.

The problems might be alleviated if teachers could borrow video tapes from resource or teachers' centres in the same way as they can obtain films, film-strips, pictures and audio-tapes. While some local education authorities do provide a video service at present, the service needs to be extended. Furthermore, it should not be restricted to recorded off-air broadcasts. It should include

IMPLICATIONS, CHANGE AND FUTURE DEVELOPMENT

tapes of a general nature which would enable a teacher to select and use only those sequences which were relevant to the children. However, very few suitable video tapes for young children in such a style are available.

It is also possible for teachers to record their own material. Small video cameras are not too expensive to buy, or could be borrowed from the local resource centre or college. Teachers could plan which modules they required, record the material and then edit it. This would be particularly relevant for video tapes of the surrounding neighbourhood with which the children are familiar, school visits, outstanding events, etc. These could then be used with the children whenever they were required. Moreover, it is not beyond the bounds of some top infants' school children to participate in the making of tapes. They can accompany teachers when filming, comment on the first takes, etc. In other words, this is acting as a further dimension not only to teachers in their attitude towards television but also to children by giving them some indication of how television pictures are made. Nevertheless, the video camera has to be procured and some guidance and assistance to teachers will probably be needed.

Although the findings do not reflect favourably on the present use of video recorders, the potential is enormous and has not been exploited. Used to its full extent, the video recorder can change the style of teaching, especially in top infants' school classes, but this is only the first development. Cable and satellite television are now being proposed but these are unlikely to become alternatives to BBC and ITV broadcasting for a very long time. Satellite channels and receiving dishes are not cheap and cabling up Britain will take a number of years, but the optical video disc is already in existence and in use in industry and higher education. It is a more flexible system than the magnetic video tape and provides greater control for teacher and children. This is stressed by Duke (1983 pp. 17-18) who states that better exploitation of the educational possibilities of television relies on the degree to which individual control can be extended when the medium is used. He contends that most broadcast programmes are ephemeral and designed as holistic units of narrative or argument without opportunities for the viewer to pause or reflect, or to take notes, without losing the thread of a programme. Since pace, level, format, structure

IMPLICATIONS, CHANGE AND FUTURE DEVELOPMENT

and language are chosen by a producer to suit the perceived average viewer, the appropriateness of any particular programme for any particular child, or group of children, is more a matter of chance than of design.

The optical video disc as an alternative to the magnetic video tape provides a new dimension in the technical ability to deliver and manipulate video sequences. The system is computer controlled and enables the computer to instruct a search for a given frame number or to play from one frame to another. Laurillard (1983) maintains that one of the main advantages of the interactive video disc for teachers is its capability to act as a vast resource of pictorial data. A video disc can store twenty minutes of motion film and still have room for a slide bank of twenty five thousand single pictures and each can be accessed and displayed within a few seconds. As few as one video disc per curriculum subject would enormously enhance a teacher's classroom resources, but a further application of interactive video is as a medium for self study.

The micro-computer has become fashionable in many infants' schools and children are working through programmes as instructed by the programme compiler. Coupled as it is to the micro computer, the video disc removes the imposition of a computer programme and through its flexibility enables a teacher to select aspects for children to tackle according to what she requires. Furthermore, as with the video recorder, some top infants' school children will be able to use the facility themselves by referring to aspects which they require. This will be achieved more quickly with interactive video than with the video recorder as the search is eliminated and replaced by the external control of the micro computer.

Interactive video extends the feasibility of both computer and television. Although the computer is a multi-purpose machine, individual programmes are designed for specific applications (Bayard-White 1985 pp. 1-8). A good computer programme may offer a learner several different routes, a number of pathways and remedial loops to aid understanding or provide assimilation, but the programme has only one destination. On the other hand, an interactive video module may be used not only for different audiences but for different purposes, i.e. a catalogue of information, a learning programme, etc. Furthermore, although computer graphics and text can be effective, movement on television can be more

IMPLICATIONS, CHANGE AND FUTURE DEVELOPMENT

illuminating. A computer programmer would take some time to produce computer graphics to demonstrate a boat sailing through water and even then the final product is unlikely to have the same impact as a film or still picture of the real thing. Interactive video has the advantage of both these technologies, offering in a single medium a blend of visual and textual information and computer assisted learning techniques. Bayard-White (loc cit) enumerates four possible uses for interactive video in schools:-

(a) As a class teaching tool by the teacher; here the player serves as a sound and picture source, providing full-length instructional programmes, short teaching sequences and reference collections of pictures and sounds, all completely controllable and rapidly accessible by the teacher.

(b) As a small group learning medium; here groups of two to four children use the disc in a relatively simple way as a tutor, responding to questions, discussing the material and learning directly from it.

(c) For individual learning; using the full interactive capabilities of a player-computer combination for direct, didactic instruction, for open-ended learning and for simulations.

(d) As a resource for data access by groups and individuals; here the disc is a library of audio and visual reference materials, accessible in many ways for many purposes.

It is problematic whether Bayard-White's suggestion that direct learning and didactic instruction could or should be attempted with young children. As indicated in Chapter 1, there is a great deal of uncertainty surrounding what young children take from television and whether they can learn directly from it. Television viewing for them has to be associated with practical activity and these aspects need to be aligned with interactive video use. Although interactive video provides further control of television material, its development for use with young children has not really begun. Its viability and usefulness in other

IMPLICATIONS, CHANGE AND FUTURE DEVELOPMENT

spheres of education are enthusiastically received, but as yet there is no material on disc for young children. However, Mably (1984) reports on a small-scale experiment with four junior schools with three programmes from the Adventure into Science - Start Here series and a programme entitled Mysteries of the Great Whales. These programmes offered a linear sequence arranged in chapters followed by an index reference section. The system was used in four basic ways: class teaching, group work, individual child use and staff development. The teachers did not see it as a replacement of their skills but as a highly usable supplement to them. They valued the rapid access to quality sound and visual information characteristic of the system because this was dynamic and did not require a high reading ability level but brought action to life before the user's eyes in a way a book could not. The teachers indicated they would like to have the system in their schools in large numbers and would be prepared to buy such systems as soon as they were available at current prices. Unlike the micro-computer, the system was considered to be friendly, needed no special training to use effectively and had wide applications for teaching at all age levels. Compared to other equivalent aids to teaching and learning, the interactive video disc was considered good value for money.

The potential for interactive video to be fully realised with young children depends on the preparation of viable discs. The development of such material takes time, is expensive and requires the advice of persons who have expertise in the education of young children. It is imperative that the material should conform to the principles of nursery and infants' school education and, in this respect, video tape material should be treated likewise. There is no likelihood of video discs becoming commonplace in schools for young children in the foreseeable future. In the meantime, the video recorder must be regarded as the most potent form of change. After all, some people may argue that teachers must prove their capability to use the video recorder effectively before progressing to the more sophisticated video disc.

REFERENCES

Bates, A.W. (1985), <u>Changing Roles</u>, The Times Educational Supplement, 1st March, p. 31.
Bates, A. (1984a), <u>Broadcasting in Education: An</u>

IMPLICATIONS, CHANGE AND FUTURE DEVELOPMENT

Evaluation, London. Constable.
Bates, A. (1984b), Spitting Image, The Times Educational Supplement, 20th April, p. 25.
Bayard-White, C. (1985), An Introduction to Interactive Video, London. Council for Education Technology.
Betts, T. (1983), Developing a Videotape Library, in "Using Video: Psychological and Social Application", ed. Dowrick, P.W. and Biggs, S.J., Chichester John Wiley, pp. 61-71.
Choat, E. (1980), Mathematics and the Primary School Curriculum, Windsor. NFER.
Duke, J. (1983), Interactive Video: Implications for Education and Training, London. Council for Educational Technology.
Jelley, C., (1984), Producing School Broadcasts for Use on Video Cassettes, paper presented to the Educational Television Association Conference, University of York, 9th to 12th April.
Laurillard, D.M. (1983), Interactive Futures, The Times Educational Supplement, 21st October, p.36.
Mably, C. (1984), Interactive Video Discs in Primary School, London. North East London Polytechnic.
O'Connor, M. (1985), Top of the Form, The Guardian, 26th February, p.11.
Ryder, L. (1985), Selling Videocassettes to Education, paper presented to A British Universities Film and Video Council Conference, London. 15th and 16th April.

APPENDIX A

LOCAL EDUCATION AUTHORITIES AND RESEARCH
GROUP LEADERS

Berkshire County Council	Mrs. P.I. Delamere, Head of Teachers' Centre, Slough.
Clwyd County Council	Mr. J.C. Evans, Headteacher, All Saints Primary School, Gresford.
Cumbria County Council	Mr. W.L. Bower, Gen. Adviser/Inspector
Devon County Counil	Mrs. M.I. Chessum, Senior Adviser, Mrs. M. Malseed, Teacher Adviser.
Essex County Council	Mr. B.A.B. Barton, Headteacher, Stanway CP School, Colchester.
Gwent County Council	Mrs. M.A. Shorthouse, Nursery/Infant Adviser Mr. P. Morton, Headteacher, Greenmeadow Primary School, Cwmbran
Hereford & Worcester County Council	Mrs. B. Garrad, Headteacher, Lickey End First School, Bromsgrove
Kent County Council	Mrs. S. Knight, Teacher, Glencoe CP Infants' School, Chatham
Lancashire County Council	Mrs. A. Allen, Headteacher, St. Mary's RC Infants' School, Leyland

APPENDIX A (Continued)

London Borough of Merton	Mrs. H. Lundgren, Primary Adviser
Norfolk County Council	Miss F. Musters, Headteacher, Easton First School, Easton
Metropolitan Borough of of Sandwell	Miss J. Mansell, Headteacher, Annie Lennard School, Sandwell
City of Sheffield	Mrs. E. Pearson, Deputy Headteacher, Abbeydale N/F School, Sheffield
London Borough of Sutton	Miss C.M. Quick, Headteacher, St. Mary's Infants' School, Carshalton
Metropolitan Borough of Walsall	Mrs. H.C. Hampton, Deputy Headteacher, Hundred Acre Wood First School, Sutton Coldfield
West Sussex County Council	Mrs. M. Mallinson, Deputy Headteacher, Southgate County First School, Crawley
Metropolitan Borough of Wirral	Mrs. M.E. Jones, General Inspector, Mrs. A. Sant, Headteacher, Glenburn Infants' School, Eastham

The following Authorities were involved in circulating the nursery questionnaire:-

Cumbria County Council (West Division)

Devon County Council (South)

APPENDIX A (Continued)

Gwent County Council

Inner London Education Authority

Metropolitan Borough of Sandwell

City of Sheffield

Metropolitan Borough of South Tyneside

APPENDIX B

INCORPORATING EDUCATIONAL TELEVISION INTO THE CURRICULUM FOR CHILDREN UP TO THE AGE OF SEVEN YEARS

<u>INTENTIONS WITH SERIES TO MONITOR</u>

Name ....
School............................ Tel. No:
Address............................
Series to be Monitored.............. <u>If possible, to be</u>
Other Series taken.................. <u>completed before</u>
Age-range of children viewing........ <u>viewing the series</u>

1. Please give your reasons for selecting this particular series:

2. Please indicate whether the Teacher's Booklet/Annual Programme Booklet has been helpful in deciding to use the series:

3. What will be the size of the viewing group and what are the reasons for this?

4. What learning outcomes for the children do you anticipate by the use of the series?

5. Any further comments you wish to make on the selection of this series?

APPENDIX C

INCORPORATING EDUCATIONAL TELEVISION INTO THE CURRICULUM
FOR CHILDREN UP TO THE AGE OF SEVEN YEARS

WEEKLY PROGRAMME MONITORING

Teacher's Name.................. School.....................

To be filled in for each programme of the selected series.
Where appropriate, delete either YES or NO or tick the
appropriate boxes.

1. Title and date of programme:

2. Please state reason if programme is not taken:

BEFORE VIEWING

3. Did you find the published material useful in any of the
   following ways? If NO please give reasons:

   (a) Background information for yourself   YES/NO

   (b) As a means of preparing the children
       for the broadcast   YES/NO

   (c) Making material in preparation for
       the broadcast   YES/NO

   (d) Any other way (please state):

VIEWING SESSION

4. Did all of the class view?   YES/NO
   If NO please state the size of the group and
   the reason for this:

VIEWING SESSION (Cont/d)

5. Did you consider the programme suitable for:

    (a) All or nearly all of the children viewing ☐
    (b) At least 2/3rds of the children viewing ☐
    (c) Fewer than 2/3rds of the children viewing ☐
    (d) None or very few of the children viewing ☐
    If (c) or (d) is ticked, please give reasons:

CHILDREN'S RESPONSES

6. Did the programme provide points which encouraged appropriate responses from the children during or immediately following the viewing session by:

    (a) All or nearly all of the children ☐
    (b) At least 2/3rds of the children viewing ☐
    (c) Fewer than 2/3rds of the children viewing ☐
    (d) None or very few of the children ☐
    If (c) or (d) is ticked, please give reasons:

GENERAL

7. Please indicate the part/s of the programme which you thought <u>particularly</u> valuable:

8. Please indicate the part/s of the programme which you thought were of little or no value:

FURTHER ACTIVITIES

9. Did you use the material provided by the programme for further activities?   YES/NO

    If NO please give reasons:
    If YES please answer the following questions:

FURTHER ACTIVITIES (Cont/d)

10. Which of the following activities did you do after the broadcast?

    (a) General discussion
    (b) Written work (including mathematics)
    (c) Art or craft activities
    (d) Other activities, please state

11. Do you intend to use the further activities as a link with the next programme in the series?   YES/NO

12. Were you able to use any of the programme content with other activities you were doing in school?   YES/NO

    If YES, was this:

    (a) Planned in advance?   YES/NO
    (b) Did it arise from the programme?   YES/NO

    Please briefly describe how the programme content was used:

13. Was the teacher's booklet useful in providing suggestions to help with further activities?   YES/NO

    If YES, please indicate which suggestions you found useful:

FURTHER COMMENTS

APPENDIX D

INCORPORATING EDUCATIONAL TELEVISION INTO THE CURRICULUM
FOR CHILDREN UP TO THE AGE OF SEVEN YEARS

SUMMARY OF TERM'S MONITORING

Name............................... Please complete and
School............................. return as soon as
Address............................ possible after the final
Series Monitored................... broadcast of the term.
Other Series Taken.................
Any Series Discontinued and....................
  reasons for discontinuation...................
                                      Age range of
                                          children.............

Delete either YES or NO and alternative answers
where appropriate

1.   Series monitored.........OFF-AIR/BY VIDEO/COMBINATION
                                    of off-AIR AND VIDEO RECORDER

2.   Do you feel that you were justified in selecting this
       particular series?   YES/NO
    Please elaborate on your answer:

3.   (a) Did you receive the Teacher's Booklet in
           good time?   YES/NO
    (b) Have you found it useful?   YES/NO
         Please explain your answer:

4.   Has the size of the viewing group changed
      since the first broadcast?   YES/NO
    If YES, please explain what changes have
    occurred:

    If NO, please state whether you would wish
    to make changes, and what they would be:

5. Have the anticipated learning outcomes for the children been achieved by using the series?   YES/NO/SOME
Please explain your answer:

6. To what extent has your involvement with the project affected your outlook towards educational television?

APPENDIX E

INCORPORATING EDUCATIONAL TELEVISION INTO THE CURRICULUM
FOR CHILDREN UP TO THE AGE OF SEVEN YEARS

The research team would like to take this opportunity to thank all participating Head Teachers and Teachers for the time and thought they have so generously given during the year. This is the final questionnaire to complete our investigation. Some similar questions may have been asked previously but some further and more detailed information is necessary to finalise our survey.

<u>CURRICULUM & LEARNING</u>

Name ....   Age range
School ....   of children............

Please delete where necessary and add explanations.

1. Please indicate how the series are viewed:
    (a) Off Air/Video/combination of both
    (b) Colour/Black and White
    (c) Number of colour television sets in school
    (d) Number of black/white television sets in school

2. What do you consider to be the advantages and disadvantages of the following ways of grouping for watching a television programme:
    (a) Whole class

    (b) Children from different classes of similar ability

    (c) Small groups

    (d) Please state which of these groupings you operate: (a), (b), or (c)

    (e) If the above is not your preferred grouping, please state why you use it

3. For people in schools with a video recorder
    (a) In what ways does your use of this differ from an "Off Air" broadcast?

(b) Would you like to use the video recorder more
extensively? YES/NO
If YES please explain

4. For people in schools who do not have a video recorder
(a) Do you feel a video recorder would be of
value in your school? YES/NO
If YES please give reasons

(b) Does your school hope to obtain a video
recorder in the near future? YES/NO

5. In what ways do you think that your experiences this
year will influence your thinking and planning regarding
the use of educational television next year?

6. Please state to what extent the Teachers' Booklets/Annual
Programme Booklets influenced your choice of series
during the past year

7. Did you discontinue to use any series during
the year? YES/NO
If YES please give details

8. Do you feel the educational television series
you have used have in the main:
(a) Supplemented and/or reinforced your
curriculum? YES/NO
(b) Directed the content of your
curriculum? YES/NO
(c) Been treated as a separate element? YES/NO
Please give reasons for your answers

9. Do you think appropriate pauses should
be made in a programme to enable a
teacher to participate in a broadcast? YES/NO

10. What kind of continuity do you consider
    desirable between programmes in the
    following areas:
    (a) Language Development

    (b) Mathematical Development

    (c) General Interest

11. Do you think appropriate pauses should be made in
    a programme to enable the children to
    participate?   YES/NO

12. What do you consider the greatest benefits
    the children obtain from viewing
    educational television?

APPENDIX F

INCORPORATING EDUCATIONAL TELEVISION INTO THE CURRICULUM
FOR CHILDREN UP TO THE AGE OF SEVEN YEARS

NURSERY TEACHERS' QUESTIONNAIRE

Name..........................
School........................
Address.......................
    .... Tel. No.................

<u>Where appropriate delete "Yes" or "No" or tick
appropriate box</u>

1. Does your Nursery Class/School have TV
   viewing facilities?   YES/NO
   If YES is this: (a) Off-Air   ☐
                   (b) By video recorder   ☐
                   (c) Combination of off-
                       air and video recorder?   ☐

2. If this facility is available do you use it:
   (a) On a regular basis   ☐
   (b) Occassionally   ☐
   (c) Not at all?   ☐

3. If you do <u>not</u> use TV please answer the following
   questions giving reasons:

   (a) Do you consider it appropriate as
       part of a Nursery programme?   YES/NO

   (b) Do you consider the available
       programmes unsuitable?   YES/NO

   (c) Do you have organisational difficulties?   YES/NO

   (d) Have you not yet considered the
       possibility and desirability of using
       TV?   YES/NO

<u>Questions 4 - 7 to be answered by those using TV</u>

4. Which series do you use?
   (Include any programme - whether Educational

TV or Children's TV)

Reasons for using:

5. Do you use TV viewing as:
    (a) A whole class activity   YES/NO
    (b) A group activity   YES/NO
        If YES please give details of
        composition of group:

    (c) In any other way   YES/NO
        Please give details:

6. Who of the following usually views with the children?
    (a) Yourself (Nursery Teacher)
    (b) Nursery assistant
    (c) Nursery student
    (d) Ancillary or parent helper
    (e) No adult

7. What benefits do you consider the children acquire from the use of TV in the Nursery?

All teachers please answer remaining questions

8. Have you any suggestions for programmes which you feel would be of particular value for Nursery children?

9. Should the occasion arise, would you be prepared to help the research team by supplying further information?   YES/NO

10. Any further comments

INDEX

activities
  creative 127
  follow-up 14
    suggestions 14, 57
  forms 52-7
  further 63
  normal 10, 34
  nursery 89
  on-going 61
  other 56, 61-70, 128
  preparation 34-5
adult
  mediator 92, 97
  understanding 3
aesthetic
  attitudes 8
  development 3
age
  annual programme guides 40
  differences 4
  taught 34
  series 31-3
Alexander, A.F. 4
Alive and Kicking
  aims 33, 59
  commencement 34
  description 33
  shortfall 34
  Spring Term 34
  teachers' booklet
    follow-up suggestions 59
    topic work 69
Amey, L.J. 9
Annan Report 2
annual programme guides
  description of series 40
  topic titles 117
  usefulness 42-3
art 35, 52, 54-5
Ayres, J.B. 16

Bailey, K. 11
Ball, S. 4
Bates, A.W. 3, 6, 7, 8, 21, 121-2, 131
Bayard-White, C. 134-5
Betts, T. 132
Blenkin, G.M. 3
Bliss, J. 6, 7, 9

Bogatz, G.A. 4
British Broadcasting Corp. 1, 18, 19, 133
  Children's Hour 85
  Children's Television 85-8, 90, 93
  policy 20
  pre-school TV series 85-8
  Radio Times 85
  School Broadcasting Council 86, 98, 125
  School Television 86
  series 71
  teacher's booklets 40-3, 44
  tradition 85
broadcasts
  integration 20
  modules 98
  off-air
    advantages 77-9
    appropriateness 71
    continuous 90, 93
    control 50, 130
    disadvantages 77-9
    editing 131
    recording 97, 131-2
    restriction 128
    timetable 20
    treatment 34
    viewing 76, 119, 120
  planned use 2, 51, 70
  programmes 98
  separate 80
Brown, D. 4
Bryant, J. 4
Bullock Report 2, 19

Calvert, S. 7
cartoons, 6, 94, 98
centres of interest
  approach 115
  back-up 14
  provision 22
  significance 3
children
  ability 46
  activities 16
  attitudes 21
  groups 46
  individuals 45-6, 105, 109, 112, 120

INDEX

interests 9, 11, 34, 55, 81
language 22
mathematics 22
play 35
pre-operational 10
reactions 70
viewers
   active 128
   passive 128
Choat, E. 5, 8, 9, 11, 12, 13, 15, 16, 19, 21, 22, 28, 29, 31, 100, 129
Cockcroft Report 2
cognition 4
college lecturers 72
Collins, W.A. 7
communication 8
Connor, R.F. 5
Cook, T.D. 5
Corder-Bolz, C.R. 6
Corteen, R. 4
craft 35, 52, 54-5
curriculum
   components 123
   considerations 3, 72, 81-3, 100, 119
   construction 22
   content 115, 124-7
   evaluation 12, 16, 129-30
   hidden 12
   institutional 12
   interpretation 11
   knowledge 12
   learning experiences 12
   nursery 90, 92
   objectives 12, 124, 130
   organisation 127
   planned 13
   principles, 22, 83
   process 3
   purpose 3
   relevance 100
   taught 12
   teaching methods 127-9

dance 57
Dean, J. 12, 18
Dearden, R.F. 2
Debes, J.L. 8
deduction

logical 5
Department of Education and Science 90, 101
development
   children's 70
   cognitive 4
   intellectual 5
   language 13, 69, 94, 101-4
   level 11, 108
   mathematics 95-6, 110-11
   mental 5
   personal 12
   technology 130-5
      material 136
   thought 5
      stages 6
discussion
   after programmes 52-3, 68, 105
   importance 101-2
   outcome 81
   over-emphasis 128
drama
   after programmes 56-7
   scheme 14
Duke, J. 133-4

Education Officers 1, 18, 19
Educational Broadcasting Council 3
educational television
   aid 2, 16, 17, 22
   change 119-36
   curriculum
      alternative 13, 81-3
      component 1, 3, 81-3
      considerations 1, 3, 14, 72, 83
      development 126-30
      directing 80
      effect on 80-3
      head teachers 15
      incorporation 11, 60, 80, 94, 128
      role 72
      supplement 18, 180
      teachers 15, 34, 70, 105
   function 69
   motivator 14
   policy 113
   previewing 19

INDEX

programmes
  activities after 51-2
  activities arising from 62-3
  availability 71
  content 41, 61, 71, 124-8, 133-4
  continuity of 60
  dissatisfaction with 113
  ephemeral 133
  gimmicks 114
  language used 108
  linking of 60-1, 108
  not taken 38-9, 109
  on-going activities 65
  other activities 61
  pace 108, 133
  questioning of 70
  unsuitable 39, 52
resource 3, 13, 14, 100
series
  aims 19, 31-3, 40, 58-9
  change 107
  choice 70
  discontinued 38
  evaluation 69
  general interest 17, 22, 68-9, 110-14, 126-7
  junior school 34, 104
  language 17, 67-8, 100-8
  mathematics 17, 65-7, 108-15
  offered 71
  policy 113
  popular 34
  selection and published material 40-4
  See also individual educational television series
stimulus 14
use
  changes in 119-36
  effective 14, 61, 69, 86, 117
  evaluation 21, 129-30
  ineffective 122, 124
  potential 71
  selective 14, 70
  whole series 14
egocentricity 9
enrichment 121-2
Essex County Council 3, 118
experience
  accumulation 65
  appropriate 65
  children's 9, 53
  direct 109
  emotional 9
  immediate 3
  intellectual 9
  past 5, 9, 10
  physical 9
  provision 17
  social 9

Fiddick, P. 17
First School Survey 2
follow-on 128
  children
    interests 11
    needs 11
  level of development 11
follow-up
  activity 14, 95
  art and craft 35
  class 21, 127
  direct 116, 121
  formal work 126
  individual 127
  integrated 70
  lessons 117
  models 35
  necessity 69
  play 57
  related 112
  structured 57-60, 128
  teachers' booklet suggestions 41-2, 58-9
  technique 11
  uniform 11, 107
  unrelated 61
Fowles, B.R. 4

Gadberry, S. 4
Goater, M. 6
Goddard, N, 11
Griffin, H. 5, 11, 15, 22, 28, 29, 100
growth

INDEX

emotional 10
mental 10
Gunter, B. 91

Haigh, G. 13
Hames, J. 19
Hannah, A. 11
harm
  pre-school children 90
  violence 90-2
Hayter, C.G. 2, 13
head teachers
  responsibility
    curriculum 15, 21-2
    educational television 15
    influence 16
    running school 15
    teachers' booklets 15
  video recorder
    acquisition 15
Henry, G. 10
Her Majesty's Inspectors 2, 72, 90-1
Himmelweit, H.T. 2
Hobart, D. 5, 11, 15, 22, 28, 29, 100
Home, A. 4, 85
home viewing 96, 119
Horner, V.M. 4
Hurst, P. 17, 21

Incorporating Educational Television into the Curriculum for Children up to the Age of Seven Years project 28-38
  age-ranges 33
  aims 28
  checklists 29, 35, 71
    replies 38
  classes
    reception 34
    top infants' 34
  monitoring 29, 38
    period 38
    results 111
  phases 26, 29, 30
  pro formas 29
  questionnaires
    language 29, 38, 100
    learning and curriculum 73
    mathematics 29, 38, 100
    pre-school children 84
    responses 78
    topic work 29, 38, 100, 116
  research groups 29
  sample 33-4, 73, 84
  sampling weeks 35
  schools
    infants' 33
    nursery 33, 84
    types 33
  series 31-4
    popularity 34
  teachers
    and curriculum 28
    attitudes 28
    involvement 69-72
    nursery 29
Independent Broadcasting Authority 1, 12, 85
  Educational Advisory Council 86, 98, 125
  topic pamphlet 117
Independent Television Companies Association 20, 49-50
Inner London Education Authority 3
Innes, Sheila 121
in-service
  courses 129
  discussions 38
  education 72, 79
  element 28-9
  school focused 79
  sessions 35, 38, 51, 73, 115, 117
interaction 4, 129
interactive
  television 119
  video 134-5
ITV Companies 1, 19, 133
  Children's Television 85-8
  pre-school series 85-8
  series offered 71
  teachers' booklets 40-3

James, C. 88
Jelley, C. 125

INDEX

Jones, C. 6

Kelly, A.V. 3
Keniston, A.H. 7
Kerr, J.F. 11-12
Kirby, N. 3

Lambert, J. 19
Language 100-8
  acquisition 96
  continuity 60
  curriculum 3, 100
  extension 68
  lessons 5
  mathematics 96
  policy 22, 68, 104
  topic work 115
  use 101
  vocabulary 21, 68, 94, 96, 101
Laurillard, D.M. 134
Lawler, L. 17, 19
Lawton, D. 12
learning
  anticipated 65
  children's 8, 21, 65
  cognitive 8
  conceptual 65
  continuous process 60
  formal 92, 96
  general interest series 65
  individual 135
  informal 93, 96
  language series 65
  mathematics series 65
  non-cognitive 8
  outcomes 65-9, 94-6
  rote verbal 4
  small group 135
Lesser, G.S. 4
Let's Read...with Basil Brush
  aim 31, 59
  description 31
  language use 103
  nursery
    use 86-8
    shortfall 34
  teachers' booklet
    follow-up suggestions 59

Levinsohn, F.H. 5
local education authorities 3, 16, 29
  inspectors/advisers 29, 72, 84
  Resource Centres 117-18, 132-3
  Teachers' Centres 132-3
  wardens 72
Look and Read 1, 11
  aims 32, 58
  description 32
  discussion 53
  duplicating masters 41
  language 67, 103-4
  linking programmes 61
  planning 63
  retention 106
  teachers' booklet
    follow-up suggestions 41, 58
    use 43-5
  written work 54

Mably, C. 136
Macintyre, A. 13-15
McCreesh, J. 3
Maher, A. 3
main survey 28-38, 84
mathematics 108-15
  acquisition 114
  change 113
  concepts 109
  continuity 60
  curriculum 3
  development 95-6, 109, 113-15
  educational television 110
  environment 96, 111
  language 96, 113
  nature 114
  notions 5
  number 95, 111, 126
  play 96, 111-12
  policy 22
  reinforcement 68, 95
  scheme 14, 22, 68, 112-13
  shape and size 111
  topic work 115
  unrelated 61
  workcards 68

INDEX

Maths-in-a-Box
    activities after programme 51
    aims 32, 59
    annual programme guide 40
    art and craft 55
    description 32
    discussion 53
    fortnightly 33
    linking programmes 61
    mathematics 110
    planning 63
    play 112
    small group viewing 47
    teachers' booklet
        follow-up suggestions 41, 59
        use 43-5
micro-computer 134
    graphics 134-5
    programme 134
Mitchell, P. 11
models 35, 55
moral attitudes 8
Morgan, M. 4
motivation 9, 16, 17, 34
Murphy, C. 88
Murray, J.F. 100
music 56, 115
My World
    aims 32, 40
    annual programme guide 32, 40
    art and craft 41
    description 32
    language 41, 104
    linking programmes 61
    mathematics 41, 110
    nursery
        declension 95, 96
        use 86-8
    planning 63
    play 57, 111-12
    science 41
    teachers' booklet
        follow-up suggestions 41, 58
        use 43-5
    unsuitability 52

National Association of Head Teachers 1

needs
    children's 9, 11, 21, 34, 115
    individual 17, 105
Noble, G. 5-6

Oakley, S. 13
O'Brien, T. 19
O'Connor, M. 121
official publications 3, 72
operations
    concrete 7
    thought 6
    pre-operational 6, 7, 9
Oppenheim, A.N. 2
Osborne, E. 10

parent/teacher association 15
perception
    auditory 18
    of programmes 106
    visual 18
physical education
    after programme 57
    curriculum 3
    scheme 14
Piaget, J. 7
play 35, 54, 57, 91, 92
Plowden Report 2
Pluckrose, H. 2
Poole, R.A. 2
preparation
    activities 34-5
    class 21
    more thorough 70
    teachers' booklets 20
    technique 11
    use of programmes 11, 34
preparation-broadcast-follow-up-technique 11, 19, 121
    detriment 60
    dispense with 128
    nursery 93
    over-emphasis 34
    pilot work 34
    video recorder 125
presenters 108
Primary School Survey 2
producers
    awareness 98, 113
    distant teachers 17, 133-4
    programme makers 125

157

INDEX

responsibility 98, 107-8
programmes
  choice 9
  content 9, 14
  incidental 9
  peripheral 9
  quantity 11
  range 28
  structure 9
puppets 6, 94, 98

questionnaire method 16

reading
  policy 22
  skills 13, 102
  teaching 115
reinforcement
  curriculum 80-1
  language policy 104
  mathematics 68
  visual 68
Reith, Lord 85
religious education
  assembly 55
  Christmas 56
  scheme 14
remembering 8
representation 10
research 17, 28, 91
resources 118, 124
  nursery 97, 124, 127
  optical video disc 134-7
rhymes/poems 94, 98, 102, 107, 126
Robinson, K. 13
Ryder, L. 122

Salomon, G. 4, 7
Salzberger-Wittenberg, I. 10
Scherer, M. 18, 20
schools
  infants' 1, 115, 136
  junior 136
  nursery 132
    assistants 93, 96
    curriculum 90, 94, 97
    part-time 85
    policy 96
    principles 88, 92, 97, 136

primary 2, 3, 12, 14, 119
secondary 13, 14, 119
science 69, 115
Seeing and Doing 1, 107
  aims 33
  art and craft 41
  description 33
  language 41, 103
  linking programmes 61
  mathematics 41
  planning 63
  science 41
  small group viewing 47
  teachers' booklet
    follow-up suggestions 41, 58
    use 43-5
  written work 53-4
Sesame Street 4, 5
skill
  acquisition 4
  basic 5
  bodily 8
  children's 21
  intellectual 8
  language 67, 101-4, 126
  listening 68, 81
  mastery 4
  perceptual 8
  reading 13, 126
  teaching 98
social
  attitudes 8
  class 4
  experience 9
  learning 12
songs
  after programmes 57
  in programmes 94, 98, 102, 126
  role 107
Sprigle, H.A. 5
Stop, Look, Listen
  aims 33
  annual programme guide 40
  art and craft 55
  description 33
  linking programmes 61
  planning 63
  teachers' booklet 41
    follow-up suggestions 58

INDEX

story
  use 43-5, 63
  unsuitability 52
story
  from programmes 52, 54
  in programmes 61, 94, 98, 102, 107, 126
Story Time 107
Sumner, H. 18, 19-20

Talkabout
  activities after programmes 51
  aims 31
  annual programme guide 40
  description 31
  discussion 53
  drama 57
  language 67, 102
  linking programmes 60
  mass viewing 48
  nursery
    use 86-8
  planning 63
  play 57
  small group viewing 47
  songs 57
  teachers' booklet 41
    follow-up suggestions 58
    use 43-5
  written work 54
teachers
  consultation with 71
  educational television
    apathy 17
    attitudes 28, 71-2, 79, 83, 121
    curriculum 10, 21-2, 122
    influenced by 18
    intermediary 10, 34, 46, 108, 128
    motivated by 18
    participation 18
    use 13, 34, 51-65, 109
  Infants' school 16, 33, 45-6
  initial training 19-20, 96, 123
  in-service education 20, 28, 97, 123-4
  nursery 33, 45-6, 84-99, 101, 132
  objectives 125

planning 61-3, 128
primary 13, 17, 132
provisions 10, 34
recording 133
re-telling story 52
role 11, 19, 65, 70-1
secondary 13, 17
teaching
  direct 4, 5, 9, 19, 63
  educational television 28, 69, 110
  evaluation 129-30
  learning 8
  mathematics 109, 110, 113-14
  method 127-9
  skills 136
  style 128
television
  activities 112
  children's responses 2
  control 135
  educational possibilities 133
  educational tool 1, 18, 130
  function 89, 96
  interactive 119
  learning from 4, 6
  movement 134
  pre-school 84-99
  power 4
  programmes
    evaluation 6
    interpretation 6
  reality 5
  receivers
    colour 15, 73-5
    monochrome 15, 73-5
    possession 73-5, 84, 97, 127
  resource 85
  role 90, 92
  use 88-9
    declension 89
The Electric Company 4
Thinkabout 107
Thomas, N. 105, 106
Thoules, R.H. 8
timetable
  convenience 76, 120
  excuses 20

INDEX

flexible 15
mass viewing 49
problems 49
topics/topic work 115-18
  Alive and Kicking 69
  class frieze 54
  continuity 60
  disconnection 61
  headings 117
  inspiration 22
  integration 69, 81
  language series 117
  mathematics series 117
  nursery 94
  planning 115-16
  provision 22
  significance 3
  time 117
Tulodziecki, G. 16

Van Hoose, J. 10
van Zon, D. 16
video camera 133
video recorder
  access 130
  acquisition 15, 20, 70
  availability 50
  children's responses 21
  class viewing 48, 120
  facilities
    fast forward 130
    pause 20, 121, 130
    rewind 21, 130
    stop/start 15, 20, 51, 120, 130-1
  feasibility 50
  head teachers 15
  individual viewing 47
  mass viewing 120
  nursery 84-5, 97
  possession 75-6
  potential 133
  quantity 3, 20, 49-50, 127-131
  recording 97
  significance 130
  small group viewing 47, 130
  topic work 117-18
  use
    adventurous 70

complacent 80
creative 75-6
flexible 21, 50
normal 50
playback 34, 47, 76, 120, 130
  implementation 50, 128
preview 15, 50, 120, 128, 130
review 15, 130
usefulness 71, 90
value 75
video tape
  cataloguing 132
  library 70, 75-6, 117-18, 120, 131
  material 128
  modules 128, 130, 133
  use 130-1
viewing
  casual 96
  facilities 19
  habit 70
  individual 47
  nursery
    means 84-5
  objectively 70
  organisation 45-51, 127
  passive 90
  practical activity 135
  teacher participation 18, 46
viewing groups
  class 17
    advantages 77-9
    disadvantages 77-9
    changes 76-80
    language 46, 48, 105
    mathematics 46, 48
    nursery 93-6
    topics 46, 48
    video recorder 48, 76-7
  mass 15
    advantages 77-9
    disadvantages 77-9
    changes 76-80
    language 48-9, 105
    mathematics 49
    team teaching 49
    vertical groups 49
    video recorder 47, 76-7

INDEX

small groups 11, 127
  advantages 77-9
  disadvantages 77-9
  changes 76-80
  nursery 93, 96
  off-air broadcasts 46-7
  video recorder 47, 76-7
Vince, P. 2
visual literacy 8
Voyat, G. 4

Wade, B. 2
Warnock, M. 91-2
Watch 1, 107
  activities after programmes 51-2
  aims 33
  annual programme guide 40
  description 32
  drama 57
  language 103
  learning 69
  linking programmes 61
  mathematics 110
  multi-ethnic unit 51-2, 57
  nursery 86-8
  planning 63
  play 57
  songs 57
  teachers' booklet 41
    children's activities 41
    follow-up suggestions 58
    use 43-5
  written work 53
Watkins, B. 7
Wellman, H. 7
Westby, S.D. 7
Williams, T.M. 4, 7
Womack, D. 113
Words and Pictures 1, 107
  activities after programmes 51
  aims 31
  art and craft 55
  description 31
  discontinued 38
  drama 57
  language 67, 103-4
  linking programmes 60
  mass viewing 48, 49
  mathematics 110
  nursery 86-8
  planning 63
  play 57
  retention 106
  small group viewing 47-8
  songs 57
  teachers' booklet 41
    follow-up suggestions 58
    use 43-5
    worksheet 41, 54
    written work 54
  written work 35, 52-4, 68, 69

You and Me
  aims 32
  description 32
  language 103
  linking programmes 61
  mathematics 109, 110
  nursery
    declension 95, 96
    informal learning 93
    popularity 90
    principles 97
    use 86-8
  planning 63
  play 57, 111-12
  small group viewing 47
  support material
    criticism 43
    rhymes 42
    story 42
    use 43-5
  unsuitability 52
  written work 53

1..2..3..Go!
  activities 54, 63
  aims 32
  art and craft 55
  commencement 34
  description 32
  discussion 53
  linking programmes 61
  mathematics 109
  nursery
    declension 96
    number work 95
    use 86-8
  planning 63
  play 111-12

INDEX

songs 57
Spring Term 33
teachers' booklet
    follow-up suggestions
      41, 59
    use 43-5
written work 54

For Product Safety Concerns and Information please contact our EU representative GPSR@taylorandfrancis.com
Taylor & Francis Verlag GmbH, Kaufingerstraße 24, 80331 München, Germany

www.ingramcontent.com/pod-product-compliance
Lightning Source LLC
Chambersburg PA
CBHW061449300426
44114CB00014B/1910